# Trust and Civil Society

Edited by

**Fran Tonkiss**
*Lecturer in Sociology*
*Goldsmiths College*
*University of London*

and

**Andrew Passey**
*Head of Research*
*National Council for Voluntary Organisations*
*London*

with

**Natalie Fenton**
*Lecturer*
*Department of Social Sciences*
*University of Loughborough*

and

**Leslie C. Hems**
*Principal Research Associate*
*Center for Civil Society Studies*
*Johns Hopkins University*
*Baltimore*
*USA*

Foreword by Ralf Dahrendorf

First published in Great Britain 2000 by
**MACMILLAN PRESS LTD**
Houndmills, Basingstoke, Hampshire RG21 6XS and London
Companies and representatives throughout the world

A catalogue record for this book is available from the British Library.

ISBN 0–333–77815–4

First published in the United States of America 2000 by
**ST. MARTIN'S PRESS, LLC,**
Scholarly and Reference Division,
175 Fifth Avenue, New York, N.Y. 10010

ISBN 0–312–23589–5

Library of Congress Cataloging-in-Publication Data
Trust and civil society / edited by Fran Tonkiss and Andrew Passey, with Natalie
Fenton and Leslie C. Hems ; foreword by Ralf Dahrendorf.
    p. cm.
    Includes bibliographical references and index.
    ISBN 0–312–23589–5 (cloth)
    1. Civil society. 2. Trust. I. Tonkiss, Fran. II. Passey, Andrew, 1963– III.
Fenton, Natalie.

JC337 .T78 2000
302.5—dc21
                                                                    00–042074

This book is printed on paper suitable for recycling and made from fully managed and sustained
forest sources.

10   9   8   7   6   5   4   3   2   1
09   08   07   06   05   04   03   02   01   00

Printed and bound in Great Britain by
Antony Rowe Ltd, Chippenham, Wiltshire

# Contents

# Foreword

On trust alone a liberal order cannot be built; we need institutions. Institutions alone cannot be sustained; we need the glue of voluntary cooperation and the anchor of belief in legitimacy. In short, we need civil society to be truly free. We need an institutional setting in which trust has meaning.

This sounds abstract, and yet it is close to our everyday experience. Consider first, trust alone. 'Take my word for it', is often a pleasing offer, especially if it is made by a friend. But in social relations, especially in conflicts, it is not enough. Political leaders have sometimes used the phrase. Indira Gandhi, when faced with campaign meetings of a million people or more, would say simple things like 'I know you are poor. I do not like poverty. I will do something about it'. She tried, but she could not prevent doubt creeping into the minds of many. In Northern Ireland, Prime Minister Blair on several occasions cut through an impasse of negotiation by saying 'I give you my word'. Again, he tried; but he too found that trust is no substitute for those firmer relationships which we call institutions.

On the other hand, just setting up institutions is never enough. It is almost too easy – as we have seen in Eastern Europe since 1989 – to create parliaments, arrange elections, and thus set up the prerequisites of democracy. Many, including Western advisers, have had a magic belief that once the institutions are there, what we call democracy, in the full sense of the word, will follow. It did not, except in a few cases where such institutions could be built on indigenous traditions. Elsewhere, people would use the paraphernalia of democracy for their own devious purposes; potential dictators to amass power, corrupt individuals to channel money into their overseas bank accounts. Weimar Germany should have been a lesson; a democracy in which people do not believe, will not last. Institutions need values which are strongly held to be sustained.

It is worth mentioning that these values cannot be replaced by economic success. It is a myth to believe that growing wealth can be a substitute for trust. (Indeed, sustainable wealth itself cannot be based simply on greed, or even self-interest; the market too needs trust, if only to give contracts credence.) If a burst of growth accompanies the establishment of liberal institutions, this may help; but the bubble can also burst as it did in the Czech Republic when Prime Minister Klaus's 'economic miracle' was revealed to be an apparition rather than a reality.

Thus democracy is fine, and so is the market economy, but the liberal order needs more. The term 'civil society' has a long tradition. For John Locke, there was barely a difference between government and civil society; his treatises deal with 'civil government'. The fathers of the US constitution a century later understood the difference. They, notably James Madison, hoped that civil society would protect people from encroachments, not just by an abstract government but even from one representing the majority. Elsewhere, notably in continental Europe, civil society has often been the refuge of those exposed to the arbitrariness of rulers. Perhaps the most desirable condition is one in which the associations of civil society supplement the institutions of governance without being either dependent on them or hostile towards them. The creative choice of non-governmental associations provides a network of trust which limits the damage which government and the state can do.

Association is the key word. People are *socii*, fellows pursuing common purposes without a constraining centre. Unfortunately there are no pleasing words to describe the most significant and effective set of associations, those of the 'third' or 'voluntary sector'. 'Sector' itself sounds organized and mechanical and in some ways untrustworthy. 'Charity' on the other hand is too closely tied to the paternalism of a bygone age. Civil society then, is the world of associations in which we rely on each other and pursue freely chosen goals together. It is the world of trust.

This volume explores many facets of this world. It is an important contribution to a debate which is going on in many countries. It leaves us with the most difficult of questions: how does one create civil societies? How do we build trust? Those of us who are concerned with helping the spread of the liberal order have often been faced with this question. Our answers are unsatisfactory. They are to some extent institutional; technical assistance for setting up

# Notes on the Contributors

**Ralf Dahrendorf** is a Life Peer, and was formerly Warden of St Anthony's College, Oxford.

**Natalie Fenton** is a Lecturer in the Department of Social Sciences, Loughborough University.

**Peter Halfpenny** is Professor of Sociology and Director of the Centre for Applied Social Research at the University of Manchester.

**Leslie C. Hems** is Principal Research Associate in the Center for Civil Society Studies at The Johns Hopkins University, Baltimore.

**David Herbert** is Staff Tutor at the Open University, Cambridge.

**Phil Macnaghten** is a Lecturer in the Centre for the Study of Environmental Change, University of Lancaster.

**Andrew Passey** is Head of Research at the National Council for Voluntary Organisations, England.

**Fred Powell** is Professor of Applied Social Studies at the National University of Ireland, Cork.

**Adam B. Seligman** is Associate Professor in the Department of Religion, and Research Fellow at the Institute for the Study of Economic Culture, Boston University.

**Fran Tonkiss** is Lecturer in Sociology at Goldsmiths College, University of London.

# Introduction

*Leslie C. Hems and Fran Tonkiss*

Questions of trust and civil society have received intense critical attention over the last decade or more, not only from academic observers but from practitioners in key areas – the voluntary sector, faith associations, public policy and welfare – where these ideas have become increasingly prevalent. Indeed the 'rate of growth' of such critical attention most probably stems from creative inter-action between academics and practitioners, exposing not only the significance but also the complexity of ideas of trust and of civil society. The purpose of this introduction is first to amplify the significance of these ideas; and secondly to provide some insight into their complexity. As part of this task it is usual for introductory chapters to essay some definitions. An important part of debates over trust and civil society, however, centres on questions of defin-ition (see, for example, Seligman, 1992: p. ix; Hall, 1995: p. 2; Salamon and Anheier, 1997b: p. 60; O'Connell, 1999: p. 9). Rather than imposing an approved form of words at the outset, the follow-ing discussion explores how these dual concepts have emerged in certain social and critical contexts. This is in keeping with the wider aims of the book. The contributors are concerned not to settle the terms of a larger debate, but to offer critical analyses of the ways these often abstract ideas play out within specific social settings: in relation to cities and citizenship; voluntary organizations; faith associations; economic relations; welfare and the state; environ-mental issues; charity and altruism.

## The 'revival' of civil society

How have ideas of trust and civil society – one a term more usually associated with private relationships, the other a theme of early modern political thought – come to be of such interest in the analysis of late modern societies? The revival of ideas of civil society partly has been a response to recent 'crises' in state forms and modes of political power: neo-liberalism and welfare restructuring in liberal democracies; the collapse of Communist structures in Central and Eastern Europe; democratic transitions in Latin America and Southern Africa; and more general anxieties concerning the role of nation-states in a global context. This re-enacts the classical split between civil society and the state – a move evident in Gellner's rendering of 'the simplest, immediate and intuitively obvious definition' of civil society as, 'that set of diverse non-governmental institutions which is strong enough to counterbalance the state, and, whilst not preventing the state from fulfilling its role of keeper of the peace and arbitrator between major interests, can nevertheless prevent the state from dominating and atomizing the rest of society' (Gellner, 1995: p. 32).

In this conception, civil society is defined by way of its separation from the state. A more substantive definition of civil society, however, might be based upon those vague but 'diverse non-governmental institutions' to which Gellner refers. In this context, civil society is given shape not only in distinction to the state, but in terms of its positive features.

In the 1980s and early 1990s, much of the literature on civil society was generated in response to events in Central and Eastern Europe (CEE). The initial focus here was on the agents of change, especially those internal agents that were oppositional or subversive in origin (for example, social movements such as Solidarity in Poland and Charter 77 in Czechoslovakia). Subsequently, the focus shifted to the pathways taken by CEE countries as they left systems of central planning and vertical command, and began to construct – with varying degrees of success – democratic structures and market economies. For different commentators, 'civil society' described, often without rigorous definition, both a key means of transition, and a desired – even utopian – end state.

kind of human association – in the shadow of the law, and in the interests of both individual liberty and collective good (see Tonkiss, 1998). More recently, the term has been used to mark out a formal 'civil society sector' (see the discussion in Salamon and Anheier, 1997b) – providing a further synonym for what is variously called the voluntary, non-profit, independent or third sector. This represents a narrowing of the category of civil society to refer to a more or less coherent sphere of non-governmental organizations (NGOs), charities, voluntary associations, social movements and the like.

If this is to emphasize 'bottom-up' structures, however, the reality of development and transition tends to be more complex and less organic. The transition process in many countries has prompted international intervention in response to both enduring and emergent problems. In certain CEE countries the social rights citizens held under communism have been eroded in the shift to a market economy, producing pronounced patterns of inequality and severe poverty – a term hardly conceptualized under the Communist system (Atal, 1999). This has necessitated international aid (as distinct from development) funding, whether from government sources or from the multitude of international charities operating in this field. While the main focus of foreign governments and international agencies has been on development, there are also examples where programmes have targeted poverty directly – for instance, the economic crisis in Bulgaria in 1997 prompted the European Union to distribute income support to families living in poverty. In other instances, foreign governments – typically operating through some supranational government body such as the United Nations (UN) or North Atlantic Treaty Organization (NATO) – have intervened in response to civil war and the atrocities of 'ethnic cleansing' that too often have accompanied political and economic transition.

The common and somewhat simplified model of transition outlined earlier – law, democracy, markets and citizens – has been considered appropriate to developing countries in almost all regions. Different societies, therefore – many with no tradition of political or economic liberalism – have been faced with the task of engendering a form of liberal civil society as part of a larger development 'package'. In some contexts, this loose category points to a focus on formulating new social systems after periods of dictatorship or government by an oppressive regime (as in Central and

Eastern Europe or Latin America). Elsewhere it relates to formulating higher societal goals than was possible within the fragmented social and political systems that frequently were part of the legacy of colonialism (as in some African nations).

Prevalent perspectives on civil society in relation to transition and development suggest that notions of civil society are closely associated with processes of change, and specifically, in moral terms, change to achieve benign social goals. If this 'purpose' is ascribed to civil society, the concept also can be applied to already 'developed' societies. Increasingly, it would seem, a range of social issues and problems – from family breakup and urban deprivation, to substance abuse and gun violence – are viewed as expressions of a deep-rooted disorder in late modern societies. For some commentators in the United States in particular, 'civil society' is seen as a balancing force when things get excessive – providing a means of regulating individual and collective behaviour without extending the powers of the state (see O'Connell, 1999). Such an approach is based on an idea of civil society as limiting the reach of government. In a more active version, the language of civil society frames government programmes for cross-sectoral and partnership solutions to a range of social and economic issues. A prominent example here is the centre-left project of a 'third way' or 'new politics' of social democracy in the United Kingdom and (to a lesser extent) other parts of Western Europe (see Blair, 1998; Giddens, 1998). Notions of civil society, that is, are used both to mark the limits of government, and as part of government strategies. In this context it is perhaps unsurprising to note the establishment and rapid growth of an international association, CIVICUS, whose goal is to promote civil society – evidence, at least, that it is not only states that are concerned to foster civil society (see Darcy de Oliveira and Tandon, 1994).

## Questions of trust

Concepts of trust also have been the focus of much critical interest over the last decade. Seligman (1997) suggests that the language of 'trust' has come to provide an alternative way of thinking about relations in civil society – relations, that is, which are freely entered, which are not compelled either by the state or by ties of family or kinship. An important catalyst for this interest in trust was provided by two publications, one by Robert Putnam (1993a) on *Making Democracy Work*, and the other by Francis Fukuyama (1996) on *Trust*. The interest aroused by these books lay in their identification of a key determinant of effective governance and comparative economic performance – social capital. Social capital, as defined by Putnam, refers to 'features of social organization, such as trust, norms and networks, that can improve the efficiency of society by facilitating coordinated actions' (Putnam, 1993a: p. 167). Social trust in this sense is not simply a value in itself, but denotes a wider facility for co-operative behaviour. Following Putnam and Fukuyama, numerous studies have linked trust and social capital to a broad set of benefits; including improved economic performance, better educational outcomes, lower crime, more effective government and the promotion of civic participation (for reviews, see Halpern, 1998; Woolcock, 1998; see also Tonkiss, below). In parallel, the communitarian arguments that developed considerable support in the late 1980s and 1990s also noted the significant role of social trust in fostering a 'spirit of community' (Etzioni, 1993).

Several national and international surveys[1] use trust as a barometer of public opinion regarding core institutions and public individuals. Levels of media and political interest in such opinion polling have intensified as consistent patterns of declining trust have emerged in different national contexts. There are clear conceptual problems here in using a deeply qualitative concept, such as trust, as the basis for rather blunt attitude statements. It is not at all obvious, for instance, that 'trust' will mean the same thing in relation to governments, to schoolteachers and to neighbours. There are also significant methodological problems – among them the lack of strong behavioural indicators of trends in social trust, and problems in establishing causality (see Putnam, 1995b; Fukuyama, 1999). Putnam works to open up the data on trust by linking these to patterns of membership in a range of associations. He argues for a strong correlation of 'trusting' with 'joining' across various social groups in the United States; even noting evidence to suggest that joining may be prior to trusting (see Putnam, 1995a; 1995b). Putnam's thesis, however, has been subject to intense criticism; both in terms of its method of 'counting' associations, and as a larger diagnosis of civic decline (see Ladd, 1996; Norris, 1996; Anheier and Kendall, 1998).

More conceptual approaches to trust have sought to delineate this idea from related notions such as faith, confidence, risk and loyalty (see Seligman, 1997; Gambetta, 1988; Giddens, 1994). For Seligman, trust is understood as 'an unconditional principle of generalized exchange unique to modern forms of social organization' (Seligman, 1997: p. 171). Trust is a distinctly modern concept in referring to relations between autonomous individuals: in his contribution to the present volume, Seligman links trust to exchanges where 'negotiation is (in the first instance) mediated by neither law, nor tradition, or religious obligations – solely by civil recognition of one another as individuals, curbing our desires (or not) in recognition of the other's preferences' (p. 15). Seligman argues that trust relationships are of a 'horizontal' nature different from such 'vertical' relationships as faith in a religious context, or obligation in a familial context (1997: p. 45). Trust between individuals translates into more general social trust, Putnam suggests, through emergent norms of reciprocity and networks of civic engagement (see Putnam, 1993a). Seligman is less sanguine. For him, trust becomes problematic in the shift from relations between individuals, to institutional and collective exchanges. In institutional settings, 'trust' tends to slide into relations of a more clearly 'contractual' nature, where legal instrument, regulatory authority or role expectation work to govern people's actions (see Tonkiss and Passey, 1999). In collective contexts, meanwhile, questions of difference and group interest often complicate assumptions that people will share 'norms of reciprocity' which guard against mistrust (see Seligman, 1997, and below).

## Conceptualizing trust and civil society

The contributors to this volume do not address civil society as a unified social 'space'. Nor do they subscribe to a narrowly sectoral definition confined to the activities of those institutions positioned 'between' state and market. Rather, ideas of civil society provide a register – at times a powerful one – for thinking about forms of association; about the encounter between individual and mutual interests; the respective limits of freedom and obligation; the conditions for collective action; the ways in which issues of self-hood and society are articulated in a public sphere. The authors engage with these themes on different levels, providing a critical framework within which to explore complex questions of trust and civil society. The first of these levels centres on the individual, and on relations between individuals.

In this context, Seligman views civil society as a concept embedded in early modern notions and conditions; translating only more or less well into contemporary settings. He suggests that, 'both trust and civil society rest on a very particular conception of the individual, an idea of the private person, imbued with moral agency and autonomy whose *civil* interaction is mediated or negotiated by something we call trust' (see p. 13 below).

Seligman takes notions of trust and civil society to refer pre-eminently to relations between individuals, and to the forms in which individual identities find public expression. In the opening chapter, he contrasts individualist and collectivist versions of civil society, discussing the real and imagined cities of Los Angeles and Jerusalem as ideal-type instances of these different forms.

Seligman's treatment of civil society is concerned in part with the way that individual interests might be reconciled with a collective good (see also Seligman, 1992). Such a perspective also is evident in Halfpenny's discussion of rational choice approaches that 'aim to model the structure of interdependencies between actors in order to demonstrate how their individual choices, freely made, jointly determine their collective outcomes' (pp. 138–9). These rather different perspectives each bear on a tension between the freedoms of the liberal individual and their relations to others in a larger civil sphere. Perspectives on civic engagement frequently centre on values of association, participation and connectedness; as well as on the practical potential of collective action (see Cohen and Rogers, 1995; Putnam, 1995b; Gutman, 1998; Giddens, 1998). A primary means through which people 'participate' in civic action, however, is through charitable giving. Halfpenny explores changing ideas of charity and altruism, arguing that trust offers only a limited means of understanding these relations, which none the less can be read in terms of larger theories of social order and individual agency.

The family provides a second frame within which to consider issues of trust and civil society. Civil society has been understood as an arena distinct from the 'public' realm of the state and the 'private' realm of the family. As such, it is held to involve different social bonds from those that are typical of these other spheres. In other accounts, however, 'the family is a basic institution of civil society' (Giddens, 1998: p. 89); and in Margaret Thatcher's famous construction, it displaces a notion of society altogether. In his contribution here, Powell indicates the tension between the 'private' family, and its construction as a public problem within welfare discourses and programmes. Within the communitarian rhetoric of recent liberal government, self-governing families represent the virtuous basis of civic life. At the same time, an image of the ungovernable family has been at the centre of policies for public order and welfare reform in a number of advanced liberal democracies.

The third construct is religion. Although religious organizations are at times seen to stand outside civil society (see Alexander, 1998), they provide an institutional presence able to sustain forms of civic association in different national and faith contexts. Rather than being organized only and fundamentally around vertical structures of authority, religious bodies and movements potentially promote horizontal relations in an extended civic sphere. Such an argument is pursued by Herbert, who critically reviews Seligman's work on the relation of trust to faith. Herbert suggests that theories of trust and civil society remain tied to liberal values of secularism and pluralism; organizations that do not fit with such a framework, none the less can be effective civic actors in such areas as education, advocacy, community-building, empowerment and economic development.

Forms of voluntary association provide the fourth context of analysis. Voluntary organizations often are taken as exemplary of trust-based relations within civil society – they also provide a focus for government discourses of partnership, and of strategies for shifting various welfare services from the state. In this context, an increasingly formalized voluntary sector is subject to growing competition, tightening regulation, and more fragile claims on social trust – these institutional dilemmas represent, as Seligman remarks, the 'Achilles' heel' of voluntary association. Passey and Tonkiss argue that the resources of trust commanded by voluntary organizations are closely tied to their formal independence and their distinctive ethos. This is complicated, however, by changing forms of governance wherein the boundaries with both state and market become harder to mark. In this light, the promotion of voluntary bodies as service providers and civic 'partners' has the effect of extending both the regulatory and the rhetorical reach of government.

Recent government programmes that put into question the boundaries between state and civil society, mirror the logic by which social movements have sought to redefine the limits of the political. Macnaghten's chapter is concerned with environmental politics as a key domain of civic engagement; a domain where civil actors contest and negotiate with government and business, and within which versions of public space are produced and struggled over. Environmental movements have been critical agents within informal politics in recent decades, challenging not only the distribution and consumption of physical resources, but also forms of state and corporate control over information (see Melucci, 1989). Questions of trust, in Macnaghten's account, are politicized in terms of public access to meaningful information about environmental risks. This provides a context for thinking in an extended way about trust as a means of mediating risk; and how this tension is played out through relations between individuals, collective movements, government and corporations.

The relation between state and civil society is the fifth level of analysis. This distinction has been crucial to ideas of civil society since the early modern period, and it casts its long shadow over contemporary debates, including those examined here. Powell considers how the state/civil society couplet has been conceived within recent political changes – in respect of neo-liberalism and welfare retrenchments in advanced capitalist democracies; and in relation to processes of socio-economic transition, especially post-Communist transition. He argues that the revival of interest in civil society has gone with a crisis of welfare state structures and of welfarist ideals. In a similar way, Passey and Tonkiss analyse how the promotion of voluntary action and provision within civil society can work as an extension of the state by alternative means.

The final frame of analysis is the economy. Tonkiss considers the different ways in which economic relations have been understood within theories of civil society – from the basis of civic association in classical liberal perspectives, to a clearly demarcated and potentially hostile domain in recent normative approaches. She examines accounts of trust and social capital as arguments for the role of social relations in shaping economic arrangements and outcomes. While forms of social capital frequently are analysed as moral as well as economic resources, her argument here is that uneven economies of social capital can work to reproduce and compound economic inequalities and privileges.

The concluding chapter explores critical perspectives on trust and civil society in the context of late modernity. Fenton addresses the complex nature of trust relations in social conditions marked by fragmentation, individualization and marketization. Rather than trust providing a basis for association within *civil society*, she argues that it offers a fragile means of mediating the dilemmas of *risk society*. If trust has been identified with the emergence of modern social relations between autonomous individuals, the systemic changes associated with forms of 'vicious modernity' can be seen to put the potential for trust into serious question.

## Note

1. The most notable international survey is the World Values Survey. In the US, the General Social Survey provides data on public trust. In the UK, the British Social Attitudes Survey has included questions of this nature, while the Henley Centre has conducted regular surveys using a standard set of questions (see Putnam, 1995b; Uslaner, 1996; 1997; Jowell *et al.*, 1997; Tonkiss and Passey, 1999).

# 1
# Trust and Civil Society

*Adam B. Seligman*

## Introduction

There can by now be little doubt that the idea of civil society has become over the past decade a much used, perhaps overused, concept. Indeed, just as the slogan arose in Eastern Europe in the 1980s as a cudgel to batter the totalitarian state, it has been taken up in the 1990s in Western Europe and in the United States by critics of the existing political order to press home their claims. Interestingly, the idea of civil society is used by political groups and thinkers on both the right and the left; and though in Europe in general it is most often the province of the left, in the United States it has been appropriated by both groups to advance their political agenda.

Thus, for right of centre and for libertarian thinkers, the quest for civil society is taken to mean a mandate to deconstruct many of the powers of the state and replace them with intermediary institutions based on social voluntarism. For many liberals, civil society is identified with social movements, also existing beyond the state. And while many of the former refuse to recognize that voluntary organizations can be of a particularly nasty nature and based on primordial or ascriptive principles of membership and participation that put to shame the very foundations of any idea of civil society, the latter are blind to the fact that the Achilles heel of any social movement is its institutionalization, which – one way or the other – must be through the state and its legal (and coercive) apparatus. In the meantime, both communitarians and liberals continue to assimilate the idea of civil society to their own terms, invest it with their own meanings and make of it what they will. Right, left and centre, North, South, East and West, civil society is identified with everything from multi-party systems and the rights of citizenship to individual voluntarism and the spirit of community (Bell, 1989; Tismaneau, 1992; Shils, 1991; Etzioni, 1993).

To some extent these contradictory usages are rooted in the concept itself. For the early modern idea of civil society emerged in the eighteenth century as a means of overcoming the newly perceived tension between public and private realms (Seligman, 1992). In fact what stood at the core of all attempts to articulate a notion of civil society in that period, and since, has been the problematic relation between the private and the public, the individual and the social; of public ethics and individual interests, individual passions and public concerns. More pointedly, the question of civil society was, and still is, how individual interests might be pursued in the social arena and, similarly, the social good in the individual or private sphere. What is ultimately at stake in this question is, moreover, the proper mode of normatively constituting society – whether in terms of private individuals or in the existence of a shared public sphere.

For if constitutive of civil society is some sense of a shared public (as maybe all would agree), so is the very existence of the private. It is after all the very existence of a free and equal citizenry – of that autonomous, agentic individual, of the private subject – that makes civil society possible at all. The public space of interaction is a public space only in so far as it is distinguished from those social actors who enter it as private individuals. Where there is no private sphere, there is, concomitantly, no public one – both must exist for sense to be made of either.

The argument presented here is that both civil society and trust rest on a very particular conception of the individual, on an idea of the private person, imbued with moral agency and autonomy, whose civil interaction is mediated or negotiated by something we call trust. To illustrate this let me begin with a story and a few examples of the most everyday type of behaviour, and from there go on to discuss two cities, Jerusalem and Los Angeles, in relation to this analysis – taking these more as icons of certain forms of social organization and less as concrete cities.

## Trust and civility

Before the prohibition of smoking in public spaces I always asked people, in line at the bank or market, if my smoking bothered them and if it did I did not light up. However when smoking began to be banned from public spaces and before it was banned from all places of work and sociability, I stopped asking the people around me if it bothered them. From my perspective the matter had been taken out of my hands, was no longer something to be negotiated by the partners to the interaction, but was now solely the function of legal and abstract dicta. Where I was legally prevented from smoking I did not of course smoke, but where it was legally permissible I stopped thinking to ask people if it bothered them. If I could smoke, I did. I was no longer negotiating the boundaries of acceptable behaviour. Freed from the burden of concern, indeed of civility, the field of smoking was henceforth ruled by law – that is, by *system* – rather than by negotiation and, what I would claim, by *trust*. Why trust? By voluntarily refraining from smoking and so circumscribing my will in favour of the interests of a stranger I was establishing in however passing, fleeting and inconsequential a manner, a social bond. I – in fact, both of us – were granting one another a measure (however infinitesimal) of symbolic credit to be redeemed at an unspecified time by a third unspecified party. Precisely this type of symbolic credit is what defines that social capital that Fukuyama (1996) and other economists identified with trust. However, as we shall see, the increasing inability of people to engage in such negotiation and trust leaves more and more realms of interaction defined solely by legal constraints which are, in their very nature, inimical to the development of trust. I have, in any case, quit smoking.

Note however the significance of the above story, which is twofold. First, its very quotidian nature, taken from the type of interaction which we engage in often in the course of the day: nothing special, nothing out of the ordinary; just the type of action and interaction that makes up the woof and weave of our daily life – sort of like queuing for a bus. Second, the fact that embedded in this seemingly simple interaction is a recognition of the actors as individual agents, responsible for their own behaviour and capable of negotiating its effects. This negotiation is (in the first instance) mediated by neither law, nor tradition, or religious obligations – solely by a civil recognition of one another as individuals, curbing our desires (or not) in recognition of the other's preferences.

Another realm where we may see this seemingly inconsequential dynamic – but one, I maintain, that is just as critical in appreciating what is at the core of a civil society – is, not surprisingly, in the rules of etiquette and civility. What, after all, is the difference between asking someone to 'Please pass the salt' as opposed to the demand 'Give me the salt'? When asking and prefacing our request with 'please' we are, however formally, acknowledging the possibility of the other to refuse. We are, in a sense, recognizing the other's agency and in so doing recognizing the other's selfhood. Any parent who has struggled to teach his child manners can, I believe, attest to just how important that recognition of selfhood is to their relationship (in this case the child's recognition of the parent as a distinct entity and not solely a function of its own interminable needs). Anyone who has been through that stage of child-rearing knows just how important a request prefaced by a 'please' (even an unmeaningful one) is. How easy it is to acquiesce to demands so phrased and how one's back goes up when demands are put in the perennial 'gimme' form.

We have internalized this type of speech over such a long period of time that we have become blind to its essential meaning, which is however clear as soon as we take time to think about it. Bracketing a request with the terms 'please' and 'thank you' is a recognition (however formal and stylized) of the contingent nature of that request's fulfilment, making of even the smallest of matters a sort of symbolic gift. It recognizes the fact that alter could have refused our request, was not in any way mandated to carry out our request, and did so 'of his own free will', as it were. Recognizing choice we thus recognize agency and in so doing, in essence, recognize the selfhood of our interlocutor. In some sense it may be claimed that the codes of etiquette are a democratization of deference: deference, once restricted to those above us in the social hierarchy, is transformed into an aspect of all (or almost all) interaction as mutual recognition becomes an aspect of modern social formations. Those same social formations which place the individual at the centre of their conception of moral agency, and around whom the terms of trust are orientated.

To be sure this democratization of deference is a salient element of that civilizing process analysed by Norbert Elias (1982); as indeed the concept of *courtoisie* is replaced in the early eighteenth century with the term *civilite*, only to be replaced in turn, by the end of the century, with the term *politesse*. Thus the embourgeoisement of courtly culture becomes the basis for modern ideas of civility and codes of mutual recognition. In Elias's terms, that inhibition of drives which stood behind the history of manners, is another form of the recognition of the other through what may perhaps be termed the circumscription of self. The whole set of developing manners charted by Elias – pertaining to the use of separate utensils by different people at table, prohibitions against putting food once bitten back in the common dish, against spitting on (later at) the common table, blowing one's nose in hand or sleeve and so on – are all no more than developing forms of behaviour based on the recognition of the other.

In fact, trust which emerges with the opaqueness of the other's will implies beyond anything else a fundamental recognition of that other personhood that is irreducible to their social roles. Trust then is a recognition of alter's agency. This is, in fact, the meaning of that freedom of the other that Luhmann (1979) refers to in explaining the emergence of trust. However, the freedom involved is not an ontological condition of existence but a socially determined and structured aspect of personality which develops most saliently (if not uniquely) in modern social formations with their increased division of labour and system differentiation. For we do not have to 'trust' in other's agency until that agency becomes a realizable potential. When most aspects of alter's behaviour can be convincingly explained (and planned for) in terms of their role incumbency, trust is not called for – confidence in systemically defined normative patterns of behaviour is sufficient (Seligman, 1997). It is only when aspects of alter's behaviour (or intentions) cannot be so accounted for, that trust emerges systemically as an aspect of social organization. Thus, and as noted by Peter Johnson, (1993: p. 79), 'To speak then, of the origins of trust is to describe the variety of ways in which agents become conscious of the freedom of others'.

As with the smoking story, the point here, with the issue of etiquette and civility, is one of recognition, of recognizing and valuing the individuality of each. What is represented in the rules of etiquette is of course a formalization of the smoking story, and – needless to add – the breakdown of such civility leads to the type of legal intervention noted at the end of that earlier story.

The whole idea of civil society – that is, of what the great eighteenth century Scottish thinker Adam Ferguson termed 'polished' society – turns on just this sort of interaction, just this sort of mutual recognition. It is the mutual recognition of individuals, no longer embedded in collective groups, no longer viewing the stranger as necessarily dangerous, no longer hostage to traditionally defined terms of membership and participation, who meet in the confines of the nation-state and, paradigmatically, of the city – that urban universe of life among strangers; among those one does not know and those who do not know you; among those who, if unknown, are nevertheless not dangerous. This meeting of self-regarding and autonomous individuals, and their mutual recognition, formed the basis of that approbation and moral sentiment which for the thinkers of the Scottish Enlightenment formed the very basis of social life – indeed, made social life possible at all.

To indulge only briefly in a quote from Ferguson (1782: p. 52):

> The mighty advantages of property and fortune, when stripped of the recommendations they derive from vanity, (or the more serious regards to independence and power,) only mean a provision that is made for animal enjoyment; and if our solicitude on this subject were removed, not only the toils of the mechanic, but the studies of the learned, would cease; every department of public business would become unnecessary; every senate-house would be shut up and every palace deserted.

Vanity here is crucial. It builds on the social nature of our existence and on our individual validation in and through the eyes of others. The public arena of exchange and interaction – the realm of civil society – is not simply a 'neutral' space of market exchange where already fully-constituted individuals meet to exchange property and develop commerce, manufacture or the arts. It is itself an ethical arena in which the individual is constituted in his individuality through the very act of exchange with others. Vanity is that which links us to the social whole as we become who we are through the other's perception of us. These individuals of Ferguson's (and Smith's) civil society were thus both emergent from group identities on one hand and, on the other, not yet eviscerated of all mutual approbation and recognition by the proliferation of legal norms and dicta – those constraints of abstract systems of communication and exchange – which define our own lives.

It is this moral valuation of the individual that has, since the seventeenth century, come to define our very ideas of the private realm as well as our evaluation of it in respect to those realms deemed more public in nature. In fact, the moral or ethical elevation of the private over the public (as that arena where virtue, morality and conscience are realized) emerged concomitantly with the growing, Western realization of individual agency and autonomy.

These conceptions stand at the core of Western liberalism as it developed from the writings of Hobbes and Locke in the seventeenth century. The sharp turn away from any Aristotelian (Christian or otherwise) conceptions of human nature (or essences) to one privileging individual responsibility and agency beyond, we may note, any metaphysically assured community of interests, stands after all at the root of what Alasdair MacIntyre (1988) has termed the 'enlightenment project' of modernity; and as such, at the core of its social categories as well – including the category of trust.

## Trust, agency and the terms of modernity

For trust to make sense, to be necessary, what is required is the free and autonomous, hence the unknowable individual. The same self-regarding self who stands at the fount of the new terms of civility and of friendship that define the modern age. For it is precisely the terms of friendship and of civility that now mediate between individuals no longer tied by long-standing, traditional and ascribed sets of obligations and responsibilities. It was this very breakup of local territorial and primordial ties that accompanied Europe's entry into the modern era, and it was this very destruction of the bonds of local and often primordial attachment to kith and kin, to territorial and local habitus, that forced the establishment of new terms of generalized trust in Western Europe and which – we should note – made the idea of the 'promise' so central to early modern political precisely that which is inherent in alter's realization of agency (were all action circumscribed by social role-expectations and normative definitions there would be no risk, only confidence or lack thereof). Trust, by contrast, implies the risk that is incurred when we cannot expect a return or reciprocal action on alter's part (which of course we could, at least within certain boundaries, when interaction is defined solely by the reciprocally defined nature of role obligations and commitments). Thus, and in Luhmann's terms, trust cannot be demanded, only offered and accepted. What it is that cannot be demanded but only offered must then be something existing beyond role-expectations which can be 'demanded'; that is, students may demand certain behaviour – or at least a certain range of behaviour – from teachers, commuters from bus drivers, store-keepers from customers, and so on. *Note*: behind the demand lies the possibility of sanctions, formal or informal. It would seem that trust – this something that cannot be demanded, only offered – is connected to that aspect of personal identity not so circumscribed by roles, that is tied to a recognition of alter's agency.

Traditional societies organized around kinship bonds were societies with very high levels of prediction, and consequently high levels of confidence based on a combination of familiarity and sanctions. Hence, to say that traditional societies (or even contemporary Japan) are societies with high levels of trust, is, it could be argued, a misnomer. They are rather societies with high levels of *confidence* based on well-known and mutually reinforced kinship obligations. Predictability is high, variability low. System (of obligations, responsibilities and mutuality) is clear and visible, and therefore confidence in behaviour is remarkably high. The corollary to this is that whatever is outside of system is totally unknown and hence dangerous. Boundaries are clear and relatively well marked and when situations arise that do not fit in to system categories – such as friendship between individuals in a system that can only 'think' in term of ascriptive, primordial categories – these are immediately translated into terms the system can accommodate – as in the phenomena of blood-brotherhood where friendship is symbolically transmuted into a primordial tie (Eisenstadt, 1956; Paine, 1970).

Modernity, if not urbanity, is of course precisely the opposite of this. It is life among strangers, among those one does not know and those who do not know you. Among those who, if not known, are nevertheless not necessarily dangerous. Interaction is risky of course – and trust as Niklas Luhmann noted, mediates risk, not danger. Unable to assume familiarity (though we constantly attempt to do so), and rooted in a 'system' of much greater cognitive lability than one based on kinship, we nevertheless enter into myriad interactions with others on the basis of something akin to trust.

True, we do not forfeit the power of sanctions in our interaction. But we would do well to recall Talleyrand's dictum that 'you can do anything with bayonets except sit on them'. The power of force, coercion, the buying off of contenders and the intractability of the collective action problem are all aspects of social order but you cannot maintain a social order over time based on just these considerations. Social order rests on something else as well. It rests on those precontractual elements of solidarity that Durkheim (1968; 1973) posited as the source of the sacred. And while this sense of solidarity has often been confused with trust we must be more subtle in our distinctions. For the basis of solidarity may indeed be different in different systems, and while some minimum degree of solidarity is necessary for a system to work, the terms of its workings will be very different in a system organized by kin exchange, one organized on the basis of a Christian ecclesia, or one on the market exchanges of autonomous self-regarding agents.

Note that the self-regarding aspect of individuals in modern capitalism is precisely what makes them strangers and hence, in some ineluctable sense, unknowable. Bernard Mandeville (1924: p. 178) well realized this when he noted that, 'Man centers every thing in himself, and neither loves nor hates, but for his own Sake'. With this a new moral basis is posited, in which '[e]very individual is a little World by itself, and all Creatures, as far as their Understanding and Abilities will let them, endeavor to make that Self happy: This in all of them is the continual Labour, and seems to be the whole Design of Life'. The shared, what Charles Taylor (1985: pp. 18–19) would deem, 'strong evaluations' of familiarity are here shattered and replaced by the morality of self-regarding individuals who, if there is to be any social order at all, any law, must in fact come to trust one another.

Contract, as the basis of social order, registers this lack of knowledge and so may well register a lack of trust also (setting up as it does the terms of confidence and predictability built on sanction), but its very emergence – especially with its gradual freedom from encumbrances in the nineteenth century – registers the triumph of that unknowable and autonomous individual among whom terms of trust *may* exist (Attiyah, 1979). It registers the emergence of those terms of personhood among which relationships built on trust become, for the first time possible on a large scale.

## Los Angeles, Jerusalem and the crises of trust

The relevance of both Los Angeles and Jerusalem to this analysis is that they represent the two extremes of what was a very fragile, eighteenth-century synthesis. In Jerusalem – again, taken more as ideal and idea than as concrete reality – collective norms, definitions and criteria of membership and participation in the collective, still determine to great extent the nature of social life. In Los Angeles the opposite is the case; there our cultural images (and indeed reality) is of a certain emptiness of public space, an evacuated civic realm, one defined by nothing more than market relations without those encumbrances to contract that have, since the late nineteenth century, been seen as defining the idea of public order or public good. It represents, indeed, the very lack of a public realm.

To begin with Los Angeles: the problem here is very much the problem of liberal individualist ideology – that is, of how to constitute a sense of community among and between social actors who are conceived of as autonomous individuals. In slightly different terms, it is the problem of a universal legal ethic which cuts at the basis of shared communality. Community or communality is always particular. And not surprisingly, most of the more popular cries for a reconstituted sense of civil society in the West stress precisely this need to reassert a sense of shared communality in the face of what is perceived as an individualism devoid of communal referents. For the more the relations between individuals are defined by abstract, legalistic and formal criteria (recall here the smoking story), the less the public realm can be defined by a shared solidarity based on concrete ties of history, ideas, love, care and friendship. The irony here of course is that these abstract laws are oriented around nothing other than the preservation of the rights, liberties and freedoms of the particular individual – whose interrelations are nevertheless lost in the web of formal rules and regulations.

In fact we seem to be losing our ability to trust to an extent proportional to our loss of the idea of the individual as anything other than a partner to market exchange (no longer – if you will – the mutual approbation of eighteenth century Edinburgh). Our increasing inability to negotiate the boundaries of interaction without involving hard and fast rules and regulations is but another manifestation of the replacement of the open-ended negotiation of trust with rule-bound and legally enforced behaviour predicated on the idea that the interaction between individuals is best character- ized as one of potential danger rather than risk. The parties to an increasing number of interactions are thus not seen as inhabiting an essentially shared symbolic, moral or ethical space. Rather they are seen as inhabiting decidedly separate, and potentially opposing or hostile, symbolic universes whose actions carry the threat of danger the one to the other. And, if danger, hence the necessity to impose strict legal codes and regulations; that is, to replace trust with strictly defined boundaries.

The very multitude of private realms, each a value in itself, can, it would seem, no longer be negotiated without the imposition of public, normatively standardized role definitions. Without a shared universe of expectations, histories, memories or affective commit- ments no basis of trust can exist. In a situation of radically incommensurate life-worlds – which is what so much of post- modern culture implies – that trust necessary to negotiate diverse expectations is lacking. What is beginning to emerge in its place is the increasingly public definitions of roles and role expectations (defined, most saliently, through the legal culture). In the absence of trust, indeterminacy becomes intolerable; hence the daily promulgation of 'speech codes', housing association regulations, smoking laws and other forms of formal regulation (and sanction) of interpersonal behaviour. This logic however goes much further than simply interpersonal relations. The world of private philan- thropic foundations in the United States is, for example, currently being reorganized to meet standards of 'diversity' and 'multi- culturalism': a subversion of their private purpose (of aiding, let us say, artistic excellence, expression and performance) in the name of currently salient public desiderata. The fact that much of this is framed in terms of collective identities (ethnic, gender or of sexual preference) is, it could be argued, indicative of the fragility of collective representation based solely on the private. It is a return to collective identities rather than individual selves as modes of representing public culture.

Whether in the emergence of new forms of family life (single parent, same sex parents, couples married for the third or fourth time), or in the new norms of 'distributive manufacturing', small-batch production, personalized payment systems and labour diversification spread out over a global market, or yet in the cultural forms of a postmodernist consciousness that abjures all 'narrative structure' and celebrates the 'porousness of experience', of 'hyper-realities', 'local determinisms' and the polymorphousness of 'particular interpretive communities', what we are witnessing is the increasing difficulty of constructing bases of familiarity and of confidence in social role and role performance that had character-ized high modern bourgeois culture (Lasch, 1995; Harvey, 1989; Lash and Urry, 1987).

The period of classical modernity was characterized by what I would call a 'strong' fit between role and person. The social actor was seen (and saw his or her self) as fundamentally constituted by the different role complexes which in turn made up the compon-ents of personal identity. This premise stood at the heart of all legal, social and economic relations and is expressed in the literature of Fielding and Richardson, and through that of Balzac, Zola and Thomas Mann. In this period, the era of the individual *par excel-lence*, the idea of the individual and the uniqueness of each rests not only on the progress of role differentiation, negotiability and reflex-ivity – but on the fact that roles were viewed (by the person and society both) as constitutive of each unique individual identity. Behind whatever front-stage was presented (at theatre, Stock Exchange, CGT meetings or Republican clubs) there stood a back-stage which was perceived of as a self, an identity, deeply rooted in one's social role complex (hence too the primacy of the private as the 'real' theatre of the self).

At present, however, the very proliferation of 'role making' (and hence of role negotiability) and the effectively infinite possibility of self-reflexive regression (through an endless array of curtains behind an endless series of stages) calls into question the very idea of the individual; that is, of that individual whose self is deemed concomitant with a relatively fixed set of role complements. We equate with the progress of modernity. In fact, it seems that much of the emphasis on multiculturalism, on the maintenance of (often ethnic) group solidarities in contrast with the prior ideology of the 'melting pot' (based on the ideology of the individual as moral absolute) are all part of this dynamic. In short, as a shared public sphere recedes from the affective grasp of the citizenry, the particular and often the private is posited in its stead as an alternative mode of symbolizing society. Ethnicity, race, gender, sexual preference, 'new age' spiritualism and so on, are thus not simply separate interests akin to corporate groups acting in the public arena. Nor are they simply what is so tellingly termed 'life-styles'. They are rather life-styles which represent a mode of identity contrary to those classic ideas of the individual that we associate with bourgeois political forms and were indeed essential to that mode of social organization. Perhaps, indeed, we will be left with those forms of political life devoid of their content. What this may mean for the organization of society is of course an open question.

Indeed, to turn to national or ethnic identities – whether in Crown Heights in Brooklyn or Hoyerswerda in Saxony: here our concern is with the organization of interest groups on racial or ethnic particular lines. More often than not, when this occurs it is seen as a breakdown of civil society and not as its realization. What such types of solidarity threaten is precisely the fundamental models of modern identity – based on the ideology of the individual – upon which modern democratic society rests. What is played out in minora in Crown Heights (between blacks and orthodox Jews) or among the neo-Nazis in Hoyerswerda is, more fundamentally, what is currently threatening the transition to democracy in East Central Europe and elsewhere. It is a dynamic whose bloody consequences were seen most tragically in the 1992–95 conflict in Bosnia-Herzegovina and the subsequent conflicts in Kosovo.

Jerusalem, then, is emblematic of a very different set of issues than is Los Angeles: not of an individualism abstracted in legal dicta and the terms of procedural justice, but, if you will, of individuals not yet fully autonomous of collective, traditional and ethnic identities – regardless of whether it is seen as a 'good' thing or not. There, in Israel, and in contrast to the situation in Eastern Europe and in certain contexts in Africa, it is not the existence of distinct ethnie whose allegiance to (and protection by) the state threatens the idea of civil society. Rather it is the idea of the state as moral community – defined in terms of the Jewish people – that poses seemingly insurmountable challenges to the existence of civil society. Why such a definition of the state in terms of the Jewish people causes different resonances from the definition of the French or Swedish State, and most especially that of the US, is of course rooted in the complexities of Jewish historical development. These include the colonial nature of the Zionist enterprise, and the continuity of strong collectivist definitions of state and society within the Jewish tradition – perpetrated by internal factors such as the overriding religio-cultural definitions of Judaism which have always stressed collective redemption rather than individual salvation as the core of their soteriological doctrines; as well as by external pressures and threats, from the 'failure of emancipation' to the horrors of the Holocaust. And, of course, the very *raison d'être* of Zionism itself is the attempt to provide for the physical security, economic well-being and cultural integrity of the Jewish individual through the reconstruction of the Jewish nation as an independent people with its own political and territorial integrity. In this process, civil self-hood (as well as state structures) became identified with and oriented around particular-collectivist rather than universal-individualist definitions of the nation-state. Complicating this ever further is the continual struggle between religious and secular definitions of the polity and of public life and space.

All this is of course but one aspect of contemporary Israel and of its historical development. Zionism also contained strong universal assumptions, rooted in its very real emancipatory claim for a new model of Jewish existence in the modern world (Cohen, 1983; Eisenstadt, 1985; Liebman and Dov-Yehiya, 1982; Avineri, 1981). The strong socialist orientation of much of pre-state Zionism bears eloquent witness to this pole of civil culture in Israel. The tragedy and pathos of contemporary Israel is that it is but one side of a seemingly intractable dilemma. For since 1967 and the continued occupation of the West Bank and the Gaza Strip, and more especially since the rise of the Likud in 1977, the early universalist assumptions which defined public life (however mediated they were in practice) have increasingly given way to an ethno-religious definition of political life and practice. These two elements stand in continual tension in contemporary Israel, and arguments can be made for either the inevitability of this tension (given the strong collectivist premises of Zionism from its inception, as illustrated for example in the notion of 'Hagshama', of individual realization through collective participation); or for its contingent and historical nature (due to the realities of the extended conflict, the occupation and so on).

The fact is that since 1967 it has become increasing difficult to mediate between these two forms of legitimation. The 1970s moreover marked a change in the terms of legitimation: the rise of the Likud and Prime Minister Begin in 1977 saw the growth of an ethnic particularism, represented in the state character awarded to certain feasts (*mimuna*) of the North African Jewish communities, the increasing tendency to equate the Holocaust with the treatment of Jews under Arab regimes, pilgrimages to different holy men and saints, and the whole rhetoric of the occupation in terms of national 'right', rather than security concerns. Most crucial, perhaps, in all this was the rise of Gush Emmunim (Block of the Faithful). Gush Emmunim came out of the religious Zionist establishment. It was a romantic movement which invoked a discourse not of law but of collective realization, messianism and divine purpose (it saw itself and was seen as the inheritor of a secular Zionist ethos of constructivism and action). At its extreme the Gush trailed off into the violent messianic Jewish underground – the terrorism against the Arab mayors, and the attempt to blow up the Mosque of Omar – an almost successful plan for cosmic cataclysm that would bring the Messiah. Yoel Nir and other perpetrators of these acts become national heroes at that time.

The period after 1982 changed much of this: the invasion of Lebanon broke the national consensus (hence the emergence of massive protest groups, the demonstration of 400,000 following the massacres in the Palestinian refugee camps of Sabra and Shatilla, the organization of conscientious objectors, the Yesh Gvual group, who refused to serve in the Lebanon invasion and then refused to serve in the occupied territories). Moreover, the fall of the USSR and the emergence of global markets provided a new impetus for both peace and market investments. What has begun to emerge is, on the one hand, global elites committed to privatization and connected to what has been termed by Samuel Huntingdon the 'Davos culture' (after the international business meetings there); and on the other hand, a localism which is often defined in terms of integral nation-alism and religious particularism. It was to a great extent this culture that murdered Rabin. We should recall the pictures of Rabin in Nazi uniform in Likud demonstrations at which Binyamin Netanyahu spoke; the threats to Leah Rabin that they (she and Rabin) would be hung up on meat-hooks like Mussolini and his mistress. We must recall as well the fact that the Rabbinic culture in the Yeshivot (religious schools) of the West Bank had developed a discourse of *rodef* and *moser* – all these highly problematic terms of Jewish religious law – to legitimize murder.

In sum, and in terms of the legitimation of society and the state, there have been some interesting developments. In a sense both sides – the universalist and the particularist – have become more extreme. With this extremism the possibility of society maintained by trust and civil interaction becomes, however, less feasible. The universalist pole rather has remade itself in the image of postmod-ern global capitalism; invoking the ideals of privatization, the devolution of the Histadrut (the National Jewish Workers Union), and the mass import of foreign workers. So much is this the case that the very idea of *avodah ivrith* (literally 'Jewish labour', one of the original goals and slogans of the Labor Zionist Movement) is, today, somewhat of a joke. Kibbutzim, when they are not leasing fields to supermarket chains, have virtually disappeared as collec-tive entities. The traditional tropes of Zionist ideology and myth, moreover, have less and less purchase on major groups in the collec-tive. On the other hand, the particularist strain has become one of integral nationalism, advocating a sacred-nationalist legitimation marked by, among other things, the rise of Shas, a political party whose ideology is that of the ethnic superiority of North African Jewish religious law over its European variants, and of a theocratic state (Fischer, 1999). So too, the boundaries have blurred between *charedim* (ultra-orthodox, non-Zionist Jews) and Mafdal (the polit-ical party of the religious Zionists), as the ultra-orthodox enter the political arena in struggles over defining the terms of collective identity in ways they never did before, and many religious Zionists for their part are fast leaving all attempts at liberal and secular discourse and legitimation (Fischer, 1996).

In a sense, then, we see that the two extremes represented by Los Angeles and Jerusalem exist within each as well. For what has

# 2
# Trust, Voluntary Association and Civil Society

*Andrew Passey and Fran Tonkiss*

*people are not people any more when they join an organisation.*[1]

## Introduction

Ideals of voluntary association are central to recent thinking about both trust and civil society. On one hand, voluntary associations are cited as exemplary forms of trust relation; on the other hand, they provide the defining features of a distinctly civil sphere (Fukuyama, 1996; Putnam, 1993a, 1995a; Cohen and Arato, 1992; Powell and Guerin, 1997). Such theoretical approaches line up with a widespread political emphasis – if often ill-defined – on voluntary action as a basis for public provision and democratic participation. A catch-all language of 'partnership' has, in this context, proved as amenable to the minimal state project of the new right, as to the declaratively 'new' politics of the liberal and social democratic left (see Taylor and Lansley, 1992; Ratgheb Smith and Lipsky, 1993; Blair, 1998).

'Trusting' and 'joining' are seen as key to processes of civic engagement (see Putnam, 1995b), and voluntary associations are a primary site for each. This link between trust and voluntary association has both intuitive and normative resonance; for that reason it can be a useful standby within political discourse, but an uncertain basis for social analysis. Our argument is that there is a gap between the fairly idealized way in which voluntary associations are imagined within debates about trust and civil society, and the way that more formal organizations operate in an institutional context. Robert Putnam makes a clear distinction between the 'classical "secondary" associations' that he sees as the basis for social trust and civic engagement, and an organized 'third sector' pursuing more instrumental and institutional ends (Putnam, 1995b: p. 666). However, it is the formal voluntary sector that bears the weight of political programmes and public expectations. Arguments that voluntary associations are not simply cradles of civic virtue are now well rehearsed (see, for example, Putnam, 1995a; Portes and Landolt, 1996; Woolcock, 1998). Our point is not to analyse the ways in which associations can be exclusionary, undemocratic or intolerant, but rather to take the discussion in a different direction: towards problems of institution and regulation. Voluntary organizations are called to account not only in terms of social values and public trust, but increasingly in terms of institutional efficiency and outcomes. In this context, they must manage a range of relations – with members of the public, client and user groups, volunteers, government regulators, corporate and public funders – that involve not simply or even primarily relations of *trust*, but also those of contract, confidence, law, loyalty and rights.

The discussion in this chapter begins by looking briefly at different perspectives on association within approaches to trust and civil society. Our concern, however, is to move beyond these theoretical debates, by engaging with the formal voluntary organizations that provide their empirical testing-ground. Here we draw on qualitative and quantitative research into voluntary organizations, both as privileged sites of trust, and as institutional proxies for ideas of 'civil society'. The first half of the discussion centres on issues of trust. While people's expressions of trust in voluntary organizations are tied to specific values and causes, they also depend heavily on the sector's independence from state and market. The second half of the discussion examines voluntary organizations as the formal infrastructure for civil society. It considers different methods for marking the limits of a 'civil society sector' (Salamon and Anheier, 1997b), before looking to the ways that individual association and participation have been integrated into recent programmes of government. Definitions of civil society conventionally work by way of a distinction with the state (see Tonkiss, 1998). However, recent governmental efforts to incorporate and direct voluntary activities and provision put such a separation into serious question. In this light, what in one sense appears as an expansion of the 'civil' sphere, can be seen as the extension of government by alternative means.

## Perspectives on association

If voluntary association has become a very prevalent concept within recent social and political debate, it is also a very tractable one. In combining vagueness with virtue it is especially well-suited to political discourse, but problems of definition trouble the theoretical literature as well. Within perspectives on civil society, a broad concept of voluntary association captures those kinds of secondary institution – charities, religious groups, unions, social clubs, campaigns, independent press, trade bodies, non-profit and community organizations – that exist 'beyond' the state (see Seligman, 1992; Tester, 1992; Cohen and Arato, 1992; Gellner, 1994; Hall, 1995; Keane, 1998). While there are border disputes over quite what is to be included in this sphere (businesses? households? the media?), there is more general agreement on the normative connotations of voluntary association. The 'washes whiter' resonance of the term picks up on values – scepticism towards state power; principles of self-help, mutualism and co-operation; freedom of association and expression – that tend to have broad political appeal and variable political uses. Voluntary or secondary associations, it follows, have been promoted as a basis for good democratic governance by communitarian, liberal and left thinkers alike; who argue in turn for their role in limiting, supporting or extending the workings of the state (see, for example, Etzioni, 1993; Putnam, 1993a, 1993b, 1995a; Cohen and Rogers, 1995).

These competing uses reflect the way that ideas of voluntary association translate into very different social and institutional forms (see Gutman, 1998). It is rather hard to avoid Alexis de Tocqueville in debates about association, so it is worth noting that he did not see the art of association as always virtuous or even useful: as he noted, American associations in the 1830s were of 'a thousand different types – religious, moral, serious, futile, very general and very limited, immensely large and very minute' (Tocqueville, 1969: p. 513). In a similar way, more recent accounts revolve around different versions of association. The simple model of free and essentially private interaction that underpins certain conceptions of trust (see Seligman, 1997; Rorty, 1996) is distinct from extended notions of 'civic community' or 'social capital' (see Etzioni, 1993; Fukuyama, 1996), which in turn contrast with more formal models of a 'third sector' (see Salamon and Anheier, 1996; Salamon *et al.*, 1998) – even though all of these might draw on a language and an ethos of voluntarism and association.

Voluntary association provides the link between ideals of trust and more formal conceptions of civil society, but has somewhat different meanings in relation to each. On the one hand, forms of voluntary association offer a model of trust relations that are closely tied to shared values, including the principle of voluntarism itself (Uslaner, 1997). On the other hand, voluntary associations provide the institutional framework for civil society. There is a gap here between voluntary *association* imagined as an ideal, and the way that voluntary *organizations* operate in an institutional environment – and it is in this gap, we suggest, that the question of trust becomes problematic. If voluntary association represents an ideal of social exchange or civic engagement (see Gutman, 1998; Putnam, 1995a), the organized voluntary sector takes in an extended range of institutional actors engaged in diverse forms of activism, advocacy and service provision (see Salamon and Anheier, 1996; 1997a; Salamon *et al.*, 1998). While values of informal association might underpin these institutional forms, voluntary organizations in practice are subject to increasing government regulation, and operate in more intensely competitive 'markets' for public trust and support. In both senses, it becomes difficult to clearly mark off a 'civil society sector' (Salamon and Anheier, 1997b) from the domains of state and business.

## Trust and voluntary association

While trust has been a keynote of recent debate about association and civic engagement, it functions as a kind of conceptual 'black box' in this context, remaining fairly unexamined on its own terms. Empirical research into questions of trust tends to rely on large-scale attitude surveys, tracking expressed levels of public trust in various social actors and institutions (see Putnam, 1995b; Putnam *et al.*, 2000; Uslaner, 1996; Jowell *et al.*, 1997). Although responses over time to a statement such as 'most people can be trusted'[2] might say something about comparative and changing public attitudes, they say very little about the nature and limits of trust relations themselves. 'Most people can be trusted' to do what, exactly? in which settings? and which kinds of people can't be trusted? Such surveys do not get at the ways in which respondents understand trust – what someone means, that is, when they claim to 'trust' each other, their doctor, government or the police.

In what follows, this more interpretive interest in issues of trust is taken up. The discussion draws on qualitative research that set out to explore the meanings people attach to 'trust'; both in a general sense, and specifically in relation to voluntary organizations (Gaskin and Fenton, 1997; Tonkiss and Passey, 1999).[3] The aim here was to open up the 'black box' in a critical way, such that the concept of trust might provide an analytic tool for thinking about different relations within and to the voluntary sector. What this research suggests is that individuals' understanding of trust in relation to voluntary organizations is strongly oriented to values, but complicated by perceptions of these agencies' behaviour as institutions. This tension, between values and institutions, provides a frame for analysing the complex ways in which voluntary organizations encounter the problem of trust.

Within this research, the voluntary sector's separation from state and market emerged as a key factor informing people's attitudes – however its distinctiveness rests not only on the sector's formal independence, but on what are seen as special values of 'care'. Such perceptions remain firmly based on traditional models of charity – conceived as help for the 'needy' or 'less fortunate' (Tonkiss and Passey, 1999: pp. 264–5). A conventional view of voluntary action, however, tends to be qualified in two ways: the first touching on questions of value, the other more clearly oriented to institutions. If the 'needy' or 'less fortunate' are constructed as deserving objects of charity, this assumption is complicated by finer judgements about legitimate *need*. Judgements here turn on questions of agency – specifically on people's perceived ability to look after themselves: while disability or illness, for instance, might be uncontroversial cases, an issue such as homelessness is not so clear-cut (ibid: p. 265). In the abstract, the voluntary sector may broadly be identified with normative values of care; but specific causes are subject to more individualized judgements of need and desert.

This common view that voluntary action should 'help the needy' or 'less fortunate people' has implications not only for the legitimacy of different causes, but also for the relationship between voluntary organizations and their users. The latter's construction as passive clients of charitable aid is sharply at odds with movements for user rights and empowerment within the sector. In recent years, service users and client groups – particularly in the fields of health and disability that are closely identified with conventional models of charity – have demanded greater voice and control within the voluntary organizations that claim to represent them (see Robson, 1996). This raises questions of how 'needs' or 'causes' are defined, and how, and by whom, organizational priorities are set. Different sets of claims may be mobilized by the trustees of voluntary organizations, the professionals working within them, and service users; and these claims are articulated in distinctive ways. In particular, user groups have taken up a language of rights to press questions of democracy, voice and accountability within organizations. The relationship of care with respect to users – if this is a primary basis for public trust in voluntary organizations – is problematized by institutional issues of power, expertise and competing interest. Efforts by user groups to secure definite claims through constitutional or contractual means might be understood as a hardening of trust relations into formal, rights-based relationships. The point is that trust, if it represents an ideal of voluntary association, is not necessarily the surest basis for a range of relationships within the voluntary sector, including those of advocacy, representation and service provision.

Such an argument opens on to questions about how priorities are set by different organizations, and the interests that these priorities serve. It links with the second way in which perceptions of trust are qualified: expressed support for charitable *values* is cut through by scepticism about charitable *institutions*. This produces some rather contradictory effects. While the dominant view of voluntary action has to do with 'raising money to help the needy' (Tonkiss and Passey, 1999: p. 264), it sits alongside resistance to an increase in fundraising requests, and to perceived pressure over giving. This ambivalence is especially clear in regard to competition between organizations, as well as in suspicions over the share taken by administrative costs and the benefits accruing to paid employees (ibid: p. 265). Views of this kind suggest that the corporate profile of many voluntary organizations may be at odds with a more basic principle of voluntarism.

## Relations with state and market

There is a tension at work here within public conceptions of the voluntary sector: organizations may initially be identified with the values that they hold and the causes that they serve, but this is complicated by their behaviour as institutions. Such issues of competition, transparency and self-interest are not limited to the voluntary sector, but inflect attitudes to public and private institutions more generally. In this context it becomes especially important for voluntary organizations to mark themselves off from other sectors, particularly in respect of government. There has been increased political emphasis in recent years, in Britain as in other national contexts, on the role of the voluntary sector in public provision and service delivery – both as an explicit policy objective and as a result of public cutbacks in such fields as welfare, housing and social services. Together with a shift to new forms of cross-sector partnership in education or health, these trends produce concerns over the precise role and remit of voluntary organizations (Tonkiss and Passey, 1999: pp. 266–7). These concerns are especially acute in relation to the overlap between state and voluntary action, and to the 'creep' in certain policy fields where voluntary initiatives are seen to account for a growing share of funding and provision (see Gaskin and Fenton, 1997; see also Ratgheb Smith and Lipsky, 1993).

Indeed, the nature of the voluntary sector's relationship to the state appears as a key determinant of public attitudes towards it. The distinctive aims and tasks of voluntary organizations, that is, become clear when set *against* the obligations of government, rather than – as contemporary political rhetoric would have it – in terms of 'partnership' with the state. Voluntary activity is seen as necessary given the absence or the failure of state provision (see Tonkiss and Passey, 1999: pp. 266–7). In a British context, such attitudes are shaped by an ethos of public welfare, where social responsibility is mediated by the state. A growing policy emphasis on voluntary provision in turn tends to be seen (accurately enough) as an effect of welfare state restructuring (ibid.). The shift in public provision from government to private and non-profit agents, involves a parallel shift in meaning from collective or *social responsibility* to *individual responsibility*. This breaks with a welfarist notion of collectivism, with the state as mediating agent, emphasizing instead the private duties of individuals. A similar tension between individualism and collectivism informs Uslaner's argument (based on data drawn from the US, UK and Canada) that 'socially conservative' views – oriented to the role of the individual rather than to that of the state – are more conducive to support for charities than is a 'social egalitarian' standpoint (Uslaner, 1996).

Problems of definition between the state and the voluntary sector are compounded by the presence of private agencies in an extended range of policy arenas – including transport, education, local government services, prisons, health, housing and urban development. In the 'semi-public' sphere that results, the role of voluntary bodies overlaps not only with that of government but with the activities of business. While businesses and voluntary organizations appear to follow rather different institutional logics (the one is interested in 'doing well', the other in 'doing good'), relations between the two increasingly are framed by discourses of partnership, mutual benefit, and corporate 'social responsibility'. The linking of private benefit to public good is evident in formal ties between businesses and charities via modes of corporate sponsorship and cause-related marketing. In these cases, the resources of public trust invested in voluntary organizations can be used to lever market share – ethical or civic values, that is, are translated into market value (see Tonkiss and Passey, 1999).

The benefits to business of these kinds of ties are fairly straightforward. However the benefits to voluntary organizations are less clear-cut. Some of this has to do with the relative power of the partners to the exchange – there are rather more good causes than there are big funders, and voluntary agencies face difficulties in securing and maintaining an equitable relationship with their more powerful business 'partner'. Moreover, research into voluntary sector funding suggests that trends in corporate sponsorship have not produced any real growth in business funding to the voluntary sector (see Hems and Passey, 1998; Passey *et al.*, 2000). Rather, business has tended to switch from direct donation to more visible forms of sponsorship – with the result that firms may promote themselves more effectively while overall levels of funding remain static.

## Resources of trust

These key relationships that voluntary organizations negotiate – with the public, with users, with government and business – provide a basis for thinking more systematically about issues of trust. Such issues play out around both questions of value and institutional factors. First, trust can be seen as the *basis for voluntary association* itself. In contrast to social relations that are mediated by contract, law or custom, voluntary association rests on trust. Thinkers such as Seligman (1997) or Rorty (1996) look to friendship and love as models of trust relations where people's behaviour is not conditioned by external agreements or by duty – rather their commitment is, in a strong sense, voluntary. Other accounts extend the concept of trust beyond these essentially private forms, seeing it as a basis for collective action in the civic sphere (Putnam, 1995a; Fukuyama, 1996; Uslaner, 1997). In both contexts, where the terms of exchange are not secured by contract or law, trust becomes a means of mediating the risks of association.

Second, trust is *linked to shared values*. If trust relations are in some sense a means of handling risk, they represent at the same time a moral decision (Uslaner, 1996). Whether in terms of religious or political beliefs, commitment to social issues, or norms of social conduct, the recognition of shared values allows people to identify with others, and to form expectations about their actions and intentions (Fukuyama, 1996: p. 26; see also Uslaner, 1996; 1997). In the context of voluntary organizations, this relates not simply to the social values attached to certain causes – anti-poverty, human rights or animal welfare – or to more general values of benevolence or altruism, but also refers to organizational values such as probity, openness or internal democracy. The linkage of trust to values is especially pronounced within research findings on the voluntary sector, showing how public expressions of trust and attitudes towards giving and volunteering are shaped by identification with values and causes (Gaskin and Fenton, 1997; Tonkiss and Passey, 1999; Hodgkinson and Weitzman, 1996; Havens *et al.*, 1998). This appears as the case both for individual motives based on personal experience or conviction (see Hodgkinson and Weitzman, 1996; Havens *et al.*, 1998), and in general attitudes to voluntary organizations regarding 'the values they hold' – where these perceptions remain fairly vague or conventional (Tonkiss and Passey, 1999: p. 264).

Third, it follows that trust represents a *moral resource* for voluntary organizations. While trust itself cannot be commodified or exchanged, it provides an intangible asset for levering support, goodwill, time and money. This point picks up on notions of trust as a 'lubricant' for action (Luhmann, 1988), a type of 'symbolic credit' (Seligman, 1997), or a form of 'social capital' that helps to secure certain outcomes (Woolcock, 1998). Rather than indicating any broad sense of generalized trust, however, here we are thinking of trust in a more narrow or instrumental way. As the 'market' for public concern, funds and time becomes more intense – whether as a result of compassion fatigue, increased competition or a punishing work culture – those organizations that have built up durable resources of trust might take the advantage in protecting and extending their market share.

If the language of commerce is an ugly one to apply to the voluntary sphere, this serves to illustrate our final point. That is, issues of trust are bound up with questions of *legitimacy*. Resources of trust depend in part on the ability of voluntary organizations and campaigns – whether Amnesty International or Médecins Sans Frontières – to claim a space that is distinct from that of government or business. The differentiation of voluntary bodies from the state and business, in ethical as well as formal terms, is an important aspect of public perceptions of the sector. In a changing political and organizational environment, however, the relationship between these different institutional actors is complex and often unclear. Attempts to integrate voluntary action into policy programmes (in such domains as unemployment, urban regeneration, health and social security), or 'cause-related marketing' on the part of business (through corporate philanthropy, affinity credit cards and the like), put into question the distinctions between public, private and voluntary sectors. While these relationships remain subject to legal and financial regulation – indeed the trend for cross-sectoral 'partnership' has been accompanied by more exacting forms of contract, accountability and compliance – the danger is that such distinctions are lost at the level of public perceptions. For a sector whose legitimacy derives in large part from its perceived independence from state and business, changing cultures of governance on one hand, and enterprise on the other, are problems to be managed as much as they are chances to be grasped.

In outlining these different takes on trust – as the condition of voluntary association, as tied to shared values, as a moral resource, and as linked with questions of legitimacy – we have traced a movement from *association* to *institutions*. This kind of slippage, we have suggested, is rather typical of debate in this sphere. Clearly, an ideal of voluntary association as an exemplary trust relation is different from voluntary organizations as imperfect institutional actors. Earlier, we referred to this problem in terms of the tension between *trust* – as an ethical relation – and *confidence* – referring to more formal relations secured by contract or other regulatory means. This tension also can be understood as one between values and institutions, between the aims of 'doing good' in an ethical sense (responding to social need, advocating for marginalized groups, speaking truth to power), and of 'doing well' in an organizational sense (securing funding, maintaining a public profile, building networks). Such a tension is captured in the truism that the point of most voluntary bodies is to do themselves out of business, even while their organizational logic seems to be to expand and entrench.

The preceding discussion suggested that the relation of voluntary organizations to both government and business shapes their ability to command 'resources of trust'. However, marking off a distinct voluntary, non-profit or 'civil society sector' (Salamon and Anheier, 1997b) from those of state and market is a difficult task, in two key ways. On one level – and given the changing governance mix in a range of policy fields – it can be hard to separate out a clearly 'independent' voluntary sector. On a different level, it is hard to 'count' association: formal organizations are far more visible than informal associations. With these caveats, the following section considers alternative ways of accounting for the formal limits of the voluntary sector.

## From association to institutions: defining the voluntary sector

If the concept of 'association' is slippery to define, it is even harder to measure. Recent debates over trends in civil association frequently turn on disputes about precisely what should be counted (see Anheier and Kendall, 1998: pp. 11–12). At a basic level, the more informal or 'spontaneous' an association, the less likely it is to show up in the figures. However, defining the limits of a formal voluntary sector is itself not a straightforward exercise. The shorthand manner of marking a 'third sector' off from those of state and market is problematic, especially given changing forms of governance which do not reduce to obvious distinctions between 'public' and 'private'. Nor does it account for the positive features of the voluntary sector itself. These problems are compounded in a comparative context. The means by which different national sectors are defined depends on several factors: how the relationship to business and government is conceived and regulated, the extent and functions of national welfare states, the legal framework within which voluntary bodies are constituted, conventions of government accounting, and so on (cf. Salamon and Anheier, 1998). Recent quantitative and comparative analysis has aimed to develop systematic definitions of the voluntary sector; seeing this not simply as a residual sphere of activity left over by state and market, but as possessing distinct formal and functional characteristics. The latter go beyond social good objectives: a trend in recent research instead focuses on the economic inputs, throughputs and outputs of voluntary organizations in specific national contexts (Kendall and Knapp, 1996; Salamon *et al.*, 1998; Hems and Passey, 1998; Passey *et al.*, 2000).

The downside of such approaches is that they tend to produce rather partial summaries of what 'counts' as the voluntary sector, which can differ markedly between studies. None of these alternative models exhaust the field either of voluntary action, or of a tertiary sector between state and market. All assume varying degrees of formalization or 'institutional presence' (Salamon *et al.*, 1998: p. 1) that discounts an extensive (and by definition incalculable) number of informal and impermanent associations. The ways in which the voluntary sector is variously defined, however, are instructive. In each case, the categories that researchers use capture something of the tension between values and institutions; as the definitions set 'public good' functions against formal institutional measures.

Hems and Passey (1998) develop an economic model of the voluntary sector in the United Kingdom limited to the definition of 'general charities' used by the government's Office for National Statistics (ONS). This relatively narrow model is geared to measuring the contribution made by charities to the UK economy. The key criteria are that general charities must be: (i) independent (constitutionally and institutionally separate from government and business); (ii) non-profit distributing (thereby excluding co-operative and mutual bodies where profits are shared between workers or members); and (iii) serve a public benefit (that is, beyond the interests of its own membership). Under this model, the operating income of the UK charity sector in 1997 was calculated at £13.1 billion (rising to £14.2 billion in 1999) while total employment included 485,000 paid workers and over 3 million unpaid workers. Gross current expenditure was set at £13.4 billion in 1999, and total assets were estimated as £65.1 billion (Hems and Passey, 1998; Passey *et al.*, 2000). General charities contributed around 0.7 per cent of the UK's Gross Domestic Product (GDP). This figure, however, does not reflect the overall contribution of the sector to national productivity, given that it fails to account for the significant impact of volunteer effort. Estimates based on the contribution of voluntary activity through direct service delivery and administration suggest that the value added figure would be closer to 1.9 per cent of GDP (ibid.).

This economic model of the charity sphere takes in 'household-name' national bodies (such as Shelter, Save the Children Fund or the Royal National Institute for the Blind), as well as local charities. By using government definitions and accounting conventions, it allows for comparison with other economic sectors and provides a basis for policy development. However, while general charities might account for a significant share of an overall voluntary sector – and tend to shape public attitudes towards it – this category excludes a diverse range of voluntary activity. It leaves out associations that feature in wider conceptions of civil society – educational establishments, trade unions, professional bodies, arts organizations, campaigning movements, social clubs, self-help and mutual societies – but officially are classed as part of the government or private sector; whose remit is seen to be limited to the interests of its members; or which are deemed 'political' in character. While this approach allows for a more precise analysis of a core segment of an extended voluntary sphere, it omits key sites of association and civic engagement – from social clubs to Greenpeace. In this way, it indicates the difficulty of accounting for a coherent voluntary 'sector' in any unitary or easily calculable manner.

At the core of the 'general charities' definition is the notion that such organizations produce some kind of *public benefit* that goes beyond their own members. This rules out organizations based on principles of mutualism – including self-help bodies, co-operatives and mutuals themselves – that otherwise might be seen as important sites of civil participation and association. As with the charity sector, research into the size, scope and nature of a mutual sector is relatively underdeveloped, in part due to similar problems of definition. Most obviously, mutual organizations often span the border between non-profit and for-profit institutions – although benefits in this case are distributed among members, rather than to shareholders.

Debates as to the state of mutualism tend to polarize around two positions. On the one hand, there has been a general 'hollowing out' of the mutual sphere, with large financial and insurance institutions converting into joint stock companies at an accelerated rate since the late 1980s. On the other hand, some analysts argue that 'grass roots' mutualism is in good health, and lies at the heart of a 'third way' in democratic governance (Leadbeater and Christie, 1999; cf. Giddens, 1998). Evidence for the latter position comes from recent British research. Taking a wide definition of mutualism – in the strong sense of organizations owned and governed by members, and in the weak sense of organizations that exhibit a more general mutual ethos – Leadbeater and Christie (1999) conclude that this sector has a membership of more than 30 million, annual turnover of some £25 billion, and employs more than 250,000 people. Rather than representing a hangover from the nineteenth century, both in terms of the mutual ideal and as an outmoded form of economic organization, mutuals can be seen to operate in the 'old' economy (in sectors such as farming), as well as in the 'new' (in information technology or e-commerce).

These surveys of the charity and mutual sectors in the United Kingdom might be compared with Kendall and Knapp's extended definition of the UK voluntary sector based on 'structural-operational' factors (Kendall and Knapp, 1996; see also Salamon and Anheier, 1996). This wider conception is built on five criteria – organizations should be: (i) formally organized; (ii) institutionally separate from the state; (iii) non-profit distributing; (iv) self-governing; and (v) based on voluntary membership and contributions (see Salamon *et al.* 1998: p. 1). Unlike the official definition adopted in Hems and Passey's study, this approach includes educational establishments, professional bodies, arts organizations, museums, and so on. It therefore produces much larger estimates of the size and scope of the sector – identified here not with charitable organizations, but with an extended conception of the non-profit sphere based on a US model. Under this definition, in 1995 the UK voluntary sector had an operating income of US$78.2 billion (around £50 billion) and employed 1.4 million people (6.2 per cent of the total workforce). The employment figure grew to 2.5 million when volunteers were included.

These UK data produced by Kendall and Knapp form part of a 22-nation study – carried out as part of the Johns Hopkins Comparative Nonprofit Sector Project – which analyses differences across the sector internationally; in terms of actual size, but also in relation to wider domestic economies (see Salamon *et al.*, 1998). Across the twenty-two nations,[4] non-profit revenue totalled US$1,150 billion, from Mexico with revenue of $229 million and Slovakia with $309 million, to the United States with revenue of $675 billion. Total non-profit employment was 18.85 million, or 4.9 per cent of total employment across the 22 nations, ranging from 8.6 million in the US (7.8 per cent of total workers) to 16,000 in Slovakia (0.9 per cent). Proportionally, the non-profit sector took the greatest share of the workforce in the Netherlands (13.4 per cent) and Ireland (11.5 per cent), and the smallest share in Mexico (0.4 per cent). Factoring in volunteers, total employment becomes 29.3 million (7.1 per cent of the total workforce). In the US, this figure increases to 13.5 million (11.9 per cent), with Mexico still at less than 1 per cent of all workers. The highest proportions of total employment again were evinced by the Netherlands (17.5 per cent) and Ireland (14.2 per cent) (see Salamon *et al.*, 1998: pp. 20–2). While the non-profit sector in the United States provided the model for this study, and appears vastly larger than those of comparator nations (accounting for more than half of total revenue, for example, and almost half of the total figure for paid employment), it might be noted that in certain other contexts (Belgium, Ireland, Israel, Netherlands), the sector takes a greater *share* of employment

While this level of financial support clearly is important to voluntary organizations, on the other side donation provides a relatively simple way for individuals to express support for certain causes, and to identify with particular values. In this manner, it represents a substantive form of 'voluntary action' which does not necessarily involve any sustained association with other people or with organizations. Rather than acting merely as an economic exchange, however, donation is based on a kind of moral calculation, and establishes (however briefly) a moral relation. As a gift that does not demand direct or immediate return, it shares in a form of generalized reciprocity that goes beyond the specific exchange. In this larger sense, the British government recently has sought to promote individual charitable giving as part of a broader programme for fostering social cohesion and civic participation – using policy measures to create a 'democracy of giving'. Here, giving is seen not simply as a financial gesture (although this is crucial to the political design), but in terms of a wider conception of civic responsibility and participation. In this deeply moralized political economy, both individual virtue and civic good are pursued by way of practices of government.

There is evidence, however, of a decline over time in public donations to the voluntary sector, both in terms of the numbers who give, and the overall value of donations (Passey *et al.*, 2000). The key area where levels of giving remain stable in the UK is in church collections – contexts where the act of donation might be seen as less than 'voluntary', but where the relationship is also more clearly premised on shared values and a sense of membership. Such a link between membership and giving is borne out by US research that maps levels of giving and volunteering against wider participation in organizations (Hodgkinson and Weitzman, 1996; see also Uslaner, 1996; Havens *et al.*, 1998). Personal networks emerge as a significantly more important factor in people's decisions to give time or money, for example, than the impact of promotions, fundraising, campaigns or appeals. Furthermore, people who are members of organizations (civic or political groups, unions, sports clubs and especially religious associations) appear considerably more likely to give time and money than do non-members (Hodgkinson and Weitzman, 1996). There is a clear sense here of how networks and associations can be viewed as forms of 'social capital' that facilitate an extended range of actions and outcomes (see Putnam 1995b).

If the act of donation involves a moral as well as an economic relation, the giving of time also can be analysed in terms of both civic and economic value. Volunteering, it might be argued, carries a greater 'cost' than does donation – the latter has an explicit money cost, but little cost in terms of time foregone. Recent approaches have aimed to account for time in quantifiable value terms: Boyle's notion of 'time dollars', for example, develops an analysis of volunteering which mirrors the approach to time developed within certain strands of neoclassical economics (see Becker, 1976). Here, donations of time earn 'dollar' values, representing not simply a symbolic, but an *actual* credit (see Boyle, 1999). Elsewhere there have been efforts to develop a protocol for auditing the economic costs and benefits to organizations of volunteering (see Gaskin and Dobson, 1996). Such projects might be seen as symptoms of an 'economic imperialism' over ways of thinking about an expanding range of social activities; however, they also indicate approaches to giving and volunteering that go beyond idealized notions of civic engagement. These forms of participation involve 'values' which are not simply social or moral in character; they can also be seen to generate economic and instrumental value.

Such instrumental values do not accrue only (indeed, even principally) to voluntary organizations. Rather, they fit with important individual motivations for volunteering. In a strong sense, the giving of time can be seen as a pristine form of altruism, which carries a high cost for the volunteer and which clearly benefits the organization. In another sense, volunteering can be understood as an exchange relation from which both parties benefit in quite 'rational' ways. Studies of the reasons people give for volunteering confirm that this decision is primarily values-based. However, it also involves other forms of calculation and interest – especially regarding skills development, work experience and employment opportunities (Davis Smith, 1998a; 1998b; Gay, 1998; Hodgkinson and Weitzman, 1996). Voluntary work carries with it, too, the non-remunerative benefits of employment – personal development, social contact, and so on. These functions of volunteering have been integrated into government initiatives – for example in the UK and Australia – that use voluntary sector placements as part of welfare-to-work employment programmes. In these contexts, voluntary organizations form part of an 'intermediate labour market' strategy in which unemployed people gain skills and experience that can be transferred into work (see Grice, 1999).

The integration of voluntary organizations into government employment programmes, or official schemes to encourage giving through the tax system, put a particular slant on notions of association and participation. Individuals' engagement with voluntary organizations is steered in line with larger government objectives: in these cases, to shift people from 'welfare to work', and to expand forms of public provision outside the conventional agencies of the state. In these contexts, certain forms of association and participation become 'governmentalized' (see Burchell *et al.*, 1991) – translated into a set of technical strategies for social and economic regulation. The incorporation of voluntary participation into new forms of governance, in this way brings into question any easy separation of a formal 'civil society sector' from that of the state.

## Conclusion

Notions of voluntary association are central to debates over both trust and civil society. However the way in which voluntary associations are positioned in relation to these dual concepts produces an immediate tension: between abstract values of trust and sociability, and more concrete institutional forms. On one hand, voluntary association represents an exemplary relation of trust. On the other, voluntary associations provide the formal architecture of a 'civil society sector' (Salamon and Anheier, 1997b). This tension between values and institutions is particularly acute at the meeting point between voluntary activity and practices of government. Civil society in principle refers to a space of association 'beyond' the state; in practice it increasingly is an object of policy. While it provides a normative category for thinking about what a 'good society' might be, a governmental version of civil society must also be realized in more substantive terms – through policies aimed at individual responsibility and the regulation of the family, and by way of an institutional sector that comes to define and formalize the civil sphere. In this move, voluntary and community organizations become the focus of policy programmes aimed at widening forms of public provision, community development and social inclusion. What on one level appears as the promotion of voluntary association and action, on another functions as a *pluralization* of government through a range of 'civil' agencies (cf. Donzelot, 1991) – less an expansion of civil society, than an extension of government.

This represents a quite distinctive and purposive use of the idea of 'civil society'. If the meaning of this term has tended to work through an opposition with the state (see Tonkiss, 1998), a revised version has been taken up within recent political discourse to denote new forms of 'partnership' between the state, the market and the social (see Blair, 1998). As opposed to marking the limits of state authority, civil society can be seen as a domain of government in two key ways. First, the delivery of public services through the voluntary sector does not simply indicate a retrenchment of government. Rather, it extends the *regulatory reach* of government through a 'semi-public' sphere of agencies. Secondly, civil society becomes a crucial arena of state legitimacy, extending government's *rhetorical reach* over themes of community and cohesion.

These processes can be spun in different ways. A formal notion of civil society is at the core of attempts to re-make social democratic politics, by means of a 'third way' or *neue mitte*. While such a politics draws on a language of trust and on ideas of civil society, these concepts are realized through the regulation of individual responsibility, and the co-opting of associations into governmental programmes. This is a potentially serious problem for the voluntary sector. If public trust and support is tied to the independence of voluntary organizations from both government and business, their integration into new forms of 'partnership' with these more powerful actors blurs such distinctions – as voluntary action comes to be directed in line with larger governmental objectives. In a deeper sense, it puts into question the idea of civil society as a means of imagining an independent and a critical space of association.

# Notes

1. Focus group member, rural unemployed young men, Cornwall. Quoted in Passey (1999: p. 27).
2. This phrasing is used in the World Values Survey – see Putnam (1995b: p. 681 n.4).
3. This research, carried out for the National Council for Voluntary Organisations (NCVO) in England, used focus group research to consider how respondents thought about 'trust' and 'confidence' in the context of social relations and institutions generally, and how they understood these concepts in respect of the voluntary sector. The qualitative study provided the basis for a larger quantitative survey examining public trust in voluntary organizations as compared to other institutions; trust in different types of voluntary organization; and confidence in organizations' accountability and efficiency. For a fuller discussion see Tonkiss and Passey (1999).
4. The 22 nations were classed as follows – (i) European Union: Austria, Belgium, Finland, France, Germany, Ireland, Netherlands, Spain, UK; (ii) other developed countries: Australia, Israel, Japan, US; (iii) Central Europe: Czech Republic, Hungary, Romania, Slovakia; (iv) Latin America: Argentina, Brazil, Colombia, Mexico, Peru (see Salamon *et al.*, 1998).

# 3
# Faith, Trust and Civil Society
*David Herbert*

## Introduction: religious resurgence and civil society

This chapter examines relationships between faith, trust and civil society, engaging critically with Seligman's ideas, and using examples drawn from a range of Christian and Muslim faith-based organizations from across the world during the last three decades. During this period there has been a resurgence of religion in the public life of societies as diverse as Iran and the United States (Beyer, 1994), Brazil and Poland (Casanova, 1994), India and much of sub-Saharan Africa (Everett, 1997; Gifford, 1998).

Religious activity in civil society, defined as 'an intermediate associational realm between the state and family' (White, 1994: p. 379) has been central to this resurgence. Religions have been particularly active in two kinds of situation. First, where the state has retreated or been unable to fulfil basic education and welfare functions, as in the cases of *Hizbullah* in Lebanon (Esposito, 1991) or base ecclesiastical communities in Brazil (Nagle, 1997). Second, where the state has repressed or undermined the credibility of more political institutions, as in Poland and East Germany in the late Communist period (Kubik, 1994; De Gruchy, 1995). But even in democracies with effective state structures, where modernization has been associated with religious decline, religions have continued and even extended their activities in civil society, as evidenced by Evangelical Christianity in the United States (Casanova, 1994), the increasing self-organization of Muslim groups across Western Europe (Shadid and van Koningsveld, 1996), and the association of religious practice with participation in voluntary work in Britain (Gill, 1992).

However, the example of *Hizbullah* in Lebanon shows that there is no unproblematic relationship between active civil society groups and democratization. Furthermore, Eastern European and Latin American examples show that while religious organizations were sometimes significant agents in 'third wave' democratic transition, their impact on democratic consolidation has been more ambivalent. Thus the concept of civil society – and especially its relationship to democratization – requires further examination, and here we turn to Seligman.

## Faith, trust and civil society

Seligman (1992) shows that since the early modern period the idea of civil society has been laden with hopes for its civilizing, democratizing and socially integrating influence. However, the inventors of the early modern concept did not envisage the extent of system differentiation and role segmentation in contemporary advanced industrial societies, and hence they incorporated assumptions about the universality of human nature and the homogeneity of communities that are unsustainable under late/postmodern conditions, and render problematic its application as a solution to the problems of contemporary societies.

Seligman describes 'trust' as 'an unconditional principle of generalized exchange unique to modern forms of social organization' (1997: p. 171), working to fill the 'gaps' between role expectations as roles diversified in modern societies. Here trust gradually replaces faith, as confidence in role expectations based on divine *fiat* is replaced by trust in man's natural universal qualities (1997: p. 44). But trust is also based on the same Enlightenment assumptions about human nature and human communities that underpin the concept of civil society. When these assumptions cease to hold good, differences can no longer be negotiated by appeal to common understandings in a shared 'lifeworld' (Habermas, 1987), but only through instrumental systems of control: here Seligman points to the increasing use of speech codes, litigation, and physical violence in American public life (1997; 1998a; and this volume). Thus we might mark a shift from a medieval world of stable roles, hierarchically organized and legitimated by faith; first to a modern world of horizontal trust relationships, and then to a late/postmodern world in which roles and boundaries must once again be codified and policed in the absence of consensus – a context which also sets the scene for the emergence of identity politics.

However, as with Habermas, Seligman may be challenged by feminists and others who argue that the image of early modern liberal societies moving towards integration through horizontal relationships of trust is misleading – verticality and exclusion persisted and even intensified during this period (Calhoun, 1993). Neither Seligman nor Habermas deny this: rather their intention is, for different reasons, to chart the emergence and decline of an ideal. Yet the neglect of this 'underside of modernity' as an ongoing feature, rather than a late/postmodern re-emergence, may none the less distort their presentations. Indeed, Foucault's (1979) argument that, from the beginning, modernity was marked by an intensification of disciplinary and surveillance practices, provides an important counter-narrative to the 'modernity as emancipation' trajectory broadly followed by both writers. This is especially important when considering issues relating to faith and faith-based organizations.

Seligman's image of faith springs from the Western tradition of political philosophy, which emphasizes features specific to the post-medieval Christian setting from which it grew. Galtung (1994) emphasizes two features of this tradition. First, 'verticality', meaning that authority for forms of interpersonal relationship tends to be conceptualized as descending 'from above' – initially from God, and later from the state – as opposed to growing 'horizontally' out of existing habits and customs. Second, a tendency toward individualization: if society is imaged as a net, this tradition sees individuals as existing in the 'knots' at the intersection between strands, in contrast to other cultural formations, in which individuals are also seen as in the 'net': 'Imagine a hunter-gatherer or pastoral-nomadic community with people woven together in structures that take the shape of rights and duties ... the more densely the net is spun, the more difficult or meaningless it will be to detach the individual from the network. Individuals are in the *net* as well as the *knot*' (Galtung, 1994: p. 6).

Of course, Seligman is not concerned with hunter-gatherers, and individualization is part of the modernizing process as systems and roles differentiate. But at least initially we need to leave open the possibility that different cultural formations may respond to this process in different ways. Certainly, religious traditions have very different starting points, and different strands exist even within the Western traditions:

> Individualising Judaism/Christianity/Islam with a transcendental god emphasises the knots, the union-oriented Hinduism/ Buddhism with a more immanent god-concept the nets. Transcendental religions endow human beings with individual souls as that which can attain union with god. Immanent religions depend less on that concept, which is rejected out of hand in radical Buddhism. But occidental religions also have immanent, net-oriented, collectivist aspects.... God also speaks through the people. (ibid.: pp. 6-7)

We have seen that Seligman's characterization of faith as a vertical relationship in contrast to horizontal relationships of trust seems to preclude the possibility that faith could promote trust. But Galtung's challenge to this vertical construction of faith opens up other possibilities. One that will be pursued here is the idea that religious traditions, including some quite conservative ones, may actually promote civility, in the sense of respect for individuals, recognition of other communities, and determination to solve differences through reasoned negotiation. In this way they may promote a general sense of trust in others in society, in Seligman's sense. This is not to say that faith cannot also lead to the opposite of civility: as this is written, hundreds of thousands of ethnic Albanians are fleeing Kosovo in the latest round of ethnic cleansing in the former Yugoslavia, legitimated not least by Serbian Orthodox religious discourse (Sells, 1996). But this disparity of evidence argues for a careful analysis of each situation, not for *a priori* rejection of faith as a possible contributor to trust and civility.

Another problem with Seligman's account is a tendency to generalize from America to the rest of the world, thus: '[T]his ... essay has been an attempt to provide the necessary background for understanding the interaction of our citizens from Los Angeles – and, by implication, the problematic meaning of civil society in all liberal individualist societies' (1992: p. 184).

However, analogies from other spheres, such as employment and production, suggest a need for caution in generalizing from

American experience. Castells (1996) has shown that the American model of post-industrialism, in which employment in manufacturing is replaced by employment in services, and which is often assumed to be a universal correlate of economic development, has not been followed by other successful advanced industrial economies such as Germany and Japan. Here much of the traditional manufacturing base has been retained, although infused with new technologies and production methods. Indeed, this example may be more than a suggestive analogy: it may be that American civic disintegration and economic transformation are part of a common process. Thus there seems to be an association between the extremes of inequality and civic disintegration found (though not exclusively) here, which Castells (1997b) links to the spatial juxtaposition of the new 'global information elite' and 'the Fourth World', or globally dispersed urban poor. However, while for Castells these new patterns of social division are indeed a global phenomenon, their severity depends both on government policy and the cultural systems through which this is mediated, thus questioning Seligman's assumption that Los Angeles represents the common destination of a logic of modernity.

Finally, Seligman's history of ideas approach appears at times to pre-empt the outcome of empirical enquiry. Thus, while at one point he distinguishes 'the concept of civil society' from 'existing social or historical reality' (1992: p. 4), restricting his concern to the former, elsewhere he draws conclusions about prospects for the latter, as when he writes: 'If within such a world it remains possible to develop a civil society, predicated on a politics of trust between individual moral agents is I think – however sadly – questionable in the extreme' (1998a: p. 19).

Partly this returns us to the problem of generalization from a specific cultural base. But there also seems to be a problem with saddling the concept of civil society with the burden of historic expectations, and then berating it for failing to perform in the demanding conditions of late/postmodernity; thus declaring that it holds no answers to the problem of contemporary societies. Instead, there would seem to be a case for running with an unencumbered concept of civil society, free from the expectation of democratic deliverance, to see what kind of effect intermediate organizations (or in this case, a faith-based subset of them) actually seem to have on civility and participation in contemporary societies.

## The conditions of liberty revisited: Islam and the social formation of civility

This chapter began with an observation that diverse civil society organizations do not necessarily have democratizing effects. State socialist East Germany provides an instructive example: it possessed a large variety of such organizations in line with north European norms, and ahead of southern Europe, yet was one of the more oppressive Communist regimes (Therborn, 1997: p. 47). Indeed, it may even be argued that the proliferation of these organizations facilitated the state's surveillance operations (through individual participation in both), without compromising their functional autonomy. Thus it is important to ask which factors shape the democratizing impact of civil society organizations. In this section we shall consider two, often stated or assumed: freedom from state involvement, and a secular, individualist ethos. Assumptions about these factors shape Western foreign and domestic policy towards various forms of civil association, so we shall also consider an example of each.

First, the relationship between state and civil society organizations. Again, an economic analogy is suggestive: the emphasis on autonomy and separation from the state in civil society discourse is paralleled in free market economics, which assumes that economic success will be inversely proportional to state intervention. However, as Castells (1996) has shown in the economic sphere, strategic government support (Japan, Germany, Korea) can be more effective than pure *laissez-faire* (Reaganite America). So it may be that the free market of ideas and associations can also benefit from some forms of state involvement. At least, one needs to be open to the possibility that this can have very different meanings in different contexts, as the examples of Turkey and the Netherlands illustrate.

Since the military coup of 1980, the Turkish state has supported the development of Islamic civil society organizations (Antov and Nash, 1999). In their internal organization these groups have tended to replicate the authoritarian structure of the state, and in this sense have not contributed to the kind of pluralization associated with many Western models of civil society. None the less, they have stimulated some developments clearly autonomous of government ideology, for example amongst women's groups, in education, in the press and other media (Özdalga, 1997: p. 83). In the Netherlands the state is also heavily committed to the financial support of independent religious organizations, following the historic precedent of pillarization (Feirabend and Rath, 1996). Here, however, the liberal character of the Netherlands state ensures a much higher degree of internal organizational autonomy. However, the very fact of plentiful state provision may be said to have produced a passive civil society. Thus state involvement may mean very different things according to the character of the state, the civil society organizations, and the interaction between them. As long as the latter have some autonomy they can exercise an independent role, while more freedom and resources does not necessarily make them more active.

Second, how important is the ethos of civil society organizations? Normative models of civil society often insist on secular and individualist orientations (for example, Gellner, 1994). Furthermore, Gellner argues that Islam is both normatively and structurally incompatible with civil society. Normatively, it cannot tolerate the effects of system and role differentiation by which different areas of society and individuals' lives increasingly function autonomously; insisting rather that all areas of life are governed by Islamic precepts, from exchange relations (for instance, the ban on usury) to sexual morality. It should be noted that this view is contradicted by Lapidus (1992), who argues that medieval imperial Islamic societies provide an alternative normative model, compatible with system and role differentiation, and historically more influential.

But Gellner does not simply argue that Islam is normatively resistant to differentiation, but also that this normative orientation coincides with social structural features which render Islam 'secularization-resistant' (Gellner, 1994: p. 14). He characterizes Muslim history until modernity as a cyclical process driven by tensions between an urban, scripturalist, 'high' Islam (further divided into lax and 'puritanical' versions), and a rural, ritualistic, ecstatic and saint-mediated 'low' version. The high version is prone to laxity and pragmatic compromise over time, but has been periodically reformed by discontented followers of the low version, invigorated by *asabiyya* (energy of tribal groups) to appropriate and attempt to implement the ideals which 'high' Islam transmitted, but never implemented. However, on achieving power such groups themselves lose touch with their tribal roots and fall into urban laxity. But modernity breaks this cycle:

> Come the modern world however – imposed by extraneous forces rather then produced indigenously – and the new balance of power, favoring the urban centre against rural communities, causes central faith to prevail, and we are left with a successful Ummah [ideal of Islamic community] at long last. This is the mystery of the secularization-resistant nature of Islam. (Gellner, 1994: p. 14)

But why should the 'puritanical' rather than lax urban Islam prevail? Gellner argues that the former has more popular appeal because while both are compatible with instrumental aspects of modernity – industrialization, urbanization, and so on – only the latter has genuine local appeal (1994: p. 23). Thus as urbanization proceeds, the puritanical high version of Islam increasingly displaces the popular saint-led version, except amongst Westernized elites.

This thesis would seem to have some explanatory power applied to societies as diverse as Algeria, Egypt and Pakistan: but Gellner too readily identifies the varieties of urban Islam with his ideal version. In practice, a variety of forms have developed, some of which have proved compatible with democracy. Thus Ibrahim comments (1997: p. 41):

> Beyond the Arab world, Islamists have regularly run for elections in Pakistan, Bangladesh and Turkey since the 1980s. In Indonesia, Malaysia, and the Islamic republics of the former Soviet Union, Islamists have peacefully been engaging in local and municipal politics ... It is important to note that in three of the biggest Muslim countries (Pakistan, Bangladesh and Turkey) women have recently been elected to the top executive office in the land ... The important thing in all these cases is that Islamic parties have accepted the rules of the democratic game and are playing it peaceably and in an orderly manner.

It is rather the *exclusion* of Islamic groups from democratic participation (as in Algeria or pre-revolutionary Iran) which engenders anti-democratic extremist reaction. Such observations at the macro level are supported by some ethnographic research. Thus Özdalga shows in her study of women students in Islamic movements in Turkey that individuals manage to combine traditional approaches to arranged marriage, feminist attitudes to the role of women in work and leadership, and revivalist Islamic attitudes to dress and public morality. In Turkish society, the relation of Islam to democratization is complex:

> ... some positive contributions are presently in the making within the press and other media (large variety of publishing houses, newspapers, magazines, and TV channels) in education (private schools of high quality ...) among women of different social standing (study circles, door-knocking campaigns, maternal and other forms of social support) and in party politics (effective grass-roots organizations). Those who close their eyes to the dynamic and pluralistic aspects of the Islamic movement, and focus only on its negative, communitarian aspects, contribute indirectly to the formation of impediments to a viable civil society. (1997: p. 83)

Dwyer's (1991) conversations with intellectuals about human rights in Tunisia, Morocco and Egypt, support this analysis. Dwyer shows the extent to which human rights discourse, contested and polysemous as it is, has penetrated contemporary Middle Eastern societies: 'Few Middle Easterners I spoke to seem ready to dismiss the idea from their cultural repertoire: they may challenge its foundations, or its provenance, or the content given it by specific groups, but the concept itself has come to constitute a symbol of great power' (1991: p. 192).

Thus Gellner's thesis on the incompatibility of Islam and civil society is too simplistic. Furthermore, these examples warn against allowing a history of ideas perspective to overshadow sociological analysis. As Özdalga argues, 'Looked up from the point of view of value judgements, it may be inconsistent to plead simultaneously for values underlying communitarian and liberal forms of organization. From a sociological point of view, however, it is fully possible to have both' (1997: p. 82).

This argument has important implications for Western foreign policy. In post-Dayton Bosnia-Herzegovina, the international community is engaged in a massive effort to reconstruct society, including civil society, along secular, Western, and democratic lines. It is important to note however, that well before Dayton many Bosnian Muslims (Bošnjaks) already identified as European and democratic, as exemplified in the writings of their political leader, Izetbegovic (1989). None the less, international funding for non-governmental organizations (NGOs) is directed primarily to organizations constructed on multi-ethnic, secular lines – hence exclusively Bošnjak or Islamic groups do not qualify. As Elissa Helms, an anthropologist who has studied Muslim women's NGOs, explains (1999: pp. 4–5):

> [I]nternational agencies ... and their implementing partners (virtually the only sources of funding for local initiatives) fund and support organizations whose proposals demonstrate a commitment to multi-ethnic and cross-entity co-operation, to the establishment of secular, democratic structures, and to respect for human rights of members of all ethnic/religious groups in all enti-ties of Bosnia ... [W]omen's organizations formed on the basis of Muslim, Bošnjak identity ... [are] mostly concentrated on educa-tive activities to strengthen women's sense of Islamic heritage and Bošnjak identity. This approach is not necessarily incompatible with Western civil society models. But the emphasis which these women's NGOs place on affirming Bošnjak and Muslim identity means that Western funding agencies do not see them as encour-aging multi-ethnicity in Bosnia – indeed they are often referred to as nationalist – and therefore do not fund them.

However it may be that without public international aid, and in spite of the equation of civility with secularism within dominant discourses of civil society, such groups are in fact doing much to promote civility, in the sense of respect for the rights of individuals, recognition of other communities, and determination to solve differ-ences through reasoned negotiation. As Helms argues (ibid.: 5-8),

> [S]ome ... have begun to combine their affirmation of Bošnjak-hood (*Bošnjaštvo*) with efforts to network with women's NGOs in

Serb and Croat areas. And, despite their continued relative isola-
tion from western-sponsored initiatives, these same groups have
begun to discuss ideas of women's rights and even feminism
without first rejecting them out of hand, weighing these ideas to
see which aspects might be applied to Bosnian society.

Ten years earlier at the opposite end of Europe, Bradford at the
time of *The Satanic Verses* controversy (1989) was another place
where 'communities were threatening to polarize into mutual
incomprehension' (Lewis 1993a: p. 118). But again, conservative
religious organizations played a constructive role in the preservation and development of civility. Philip Lewis, the Anglican
bishop's inter-faith adviser, describes how the bishop organized
meetings, first with representatives from all Bradford's faith
communities, and then between Muslims, civic leaders, politicians
and the police, using the safe haven of the rural diocesan retreat
centre. These meetings permitted the constructive channelling of
frustration felt by different parties, and by recognizing Muslims'
views may have helped the Council of Mosques decide to terminate
public demonstrations.

The bishop's action here, in facilitating dialogue primarily
between male elites, is subject to Yasmin Ali's criticism that British
multiculturalist politics excludes women and other less powerful
groups by fusing 'Subcontinental systems of patronage and obligation ... with British traditions of representation without democratic
accountability' (Ali, 1992: p. 110). But at least the bishop was able
to act at a time when secular organizations were paralysed. As Lewis
shows, community relations organizations and political parties
were split between liberal loyalties to free speech and a desire to
support an outraged minority (Lewis, 1993b). The neglect of religious factors in the community relations literature, which at this
time was mostly structured around the concept of 'race', cannot
have helped here (Herbert, 1997). The mediating role of the bishop
also points to the broader civil society function of religious organizations in truth and reconciliation commissions in new
democracies, both in South Africa and Latin America.

Such examples provide a context for the reconsideration of relationships between faith, trust and civil society. For Seligman trust is
defined in contrast to faith in an almost social evolutionary scheme,

in which the unconditionality of trust in God is replaced by that of trust in man (1997: p. 44), so that 'we are all a society of atheists now' (ibid.: p. 45). This phrase jars with the evidence we have considered. Taken literally, it is simply not true; but Seligman's writing on Israel shows him to be fully aware of the contemporary vitality of faith groups, so what does he mean? Perhaps that modern societies can no longer be held together by a common belief in God. But the declining domination of any one tradition does not mean that faith communities, under late/postmodern conditions, may not contribute to social integration in new ways.

In pre-modern societies, religious pluralism was dealt with by subordinating minority groups – hence the Roman Empire's general insistence on sacrifice to the Emperor cult, the subordination of Jews and Christians in the Ottoman *millet* system, and the absorption of Muslims and Christians into subordinate roles in the Hindu caste system. Under modern conditions increased social mobility and correlative developments in political thought mean that this solution is neither practically nor ideologically possible. So religion as a top-down system of societal integration becomes unviable. But this leaves open the possibility that a diversity of faith communities may, under some conditions, contribute to the promotion of trust, both through the horizontal networks of trusting relationships which they foster within themselves, and more widely through universalist aspects of their ethical systems ('love your neighbour as yourself' and so on). Indeed, this is the vision of Rabbi Jonathon Sacks as outlined in his Reith Lectures on *The Persistence of Faith* (1990–91), and developed by in a sociological direction by the Christian theologian Robin Gill (1992).

## Religious communities, secularization and civility

Sacks contends that the basic problem of modern social life lies 'not with our economic and political systems, but in a certain emptiness at the heart of our common life' (1990–91: p. 4). He argues that religions have a substantial contribution to make to solving this problem, specifically by 'creating communities', and by 'charting our shared moral landscape, that sense of a common good that we need if our communities are to cohere as a society' (1990–91: p. 10). But given the differences between religions, and the large number of people who do not follow any of them, how can religions do this? Sacks' answer is through the promotion of common values, such as shared responsibility, mutual support, and fidelity in relationships. While these are shared more widely across society (though undermined by social fragmentation), they are specifically nurtured by religious communities, who promote them in the wider society through participation in public life. Thus Sacks begins to respond to the criticism that communitarians fail to explain how virtues nurtured by small communities can be transposed on to whole societies (Nino, 1989).

This response is developed by Gill, who shows that religious communities help to sustain practices of 'caring beyond self-interest' (1992: p. 1) in contemporary British society. For example, Gerard (in Abrams *et al.*, 1985) found that involvement in voluntary work correlated strongly and positively with religious commitment. Thus: '... roughly half of those in the highest category on the combined scale undertook voluntary work; almost nine tenths of those on the lowest category undertook none at all' (Abrams *et al.*, 1985: p. 84).

Indeed, regular attendance at Christian worship emerged as the single most significant predictor of engagement in voluntary work, ahead of social class or education, findings broadly supported by the European Values Systems surveys (Gill, 1992: pp. 19–20). Similar evidence for the links between religious observance, charitable giving and volunteering, has appeared in a number of US studies (Jackson *et al.*, 1995; Hodgkinson and Weitzman, 1996; Schervisch and Havens, 1997; Sargeant, 1999). Gill (1992: pp. 81–2) suggests that the reason for this association lies in the role of worship in religious communities:

> For Judaism, Christianity and Islam it is worship that provides the link that I believe is especially crucial for effective care in society – the link between logic and structures. Within each of these traditions individuals who believe in theory there is a God who cares (and who encourages them to care) are confronted in worship with this caring God ... any care we that we show to others has already been shown to us by a God who cares. Goodness beyond self-interest is identified as the true *telos* of a world created by a God who acted and continues to act in creation beyond self-interest.

Religious communities may fail to live up to such values, but in their worship they continue to transmit them. Understanding of the social processes at work here can be strengthened by using virtue ethics. In contrast to other traditions of ethics, this approach emphasizes character formation, focusing attention on the differential development of individuals and the social conditions under which this takes place, including the role of families, communities, and other social institutions (Herbert, 2000).

However, some theories of secularization suggest that the ability of a religious community to grow and sustain itself may be adversely affected by the participation of its members in public activities. Religious belief may provide 'start-up capital' for participation, but cannot replenish itself, so members become absorbed in the secular mainstream and lose their religious identity. Here Gill cites Wilson's work on sectarianism, which suggests that those groups which erect the most rigid boundaries around their communities, confining charity to themselves or potential converts, best sustain their memberships. In contrast, '... once a sect does genuinely attempt to influence society especially in areas of care – the Salvation Army today is an obvious example – it soon becomes denominationalised in the process. By taking this step, so Wilson argues, such a sect is likely to become secularized itself' (Gill, 1992: pp. 69–70).

In response, Gill points to alternative forms of engagement with society – individual, prophetic, inter-church and transposing church. The first two refer to individuals or alliances, the latter often run across denominations and mobilize around a single issue or cluster of issues – Christian CND or pro-life movements are examples. The 'transposing church' transforms society by the diffusion – and often mutation in the process – of Christian ideas and values, as with Weber's Protestant ethic thesis, or Mestrovic's argument that Catholicism has a positive role in preserving 'culture, community and non-utilitarian individualism' (1993: p. 109). However, while such models aid thinking about how religion may continue to influence society, they fail to address Wilson's problem of declining returns. To do this, we must turn to Casanova's (1994) reformulation of the secularization thesis.

Casanova argues that secularization consists of three related but distinct processes. First, the differentiation of modern societies into semi-autonomous spheres, involving the freeing of secular spheres from religious institutions and norms. Second, the decline of religious beliefs and practices, and third, the marginalization of religion into a privatized sphere. While the first is an inevitable part of the process of modernization, decline and privatization of religion do not necessarily follow, but rather are contingent consequences dependent on other factors, including the response to differentiation of religious communities themselves. Casanova contends that in the United States, Brazil and Poland decline has not followed from differentiation, although he also considers the counter-example of Spain. He divides the public sphere into state, political society, and civil society, arguing that while church power in the first two is ultimately incompatible with democratic modernity, a public role in civil society appears to be sustainable. Thus if churches learn to embrace differentiation, supporting democracy and accepting a new role as one voice amongst many in civil society, undergirding this public voice with pastoral and voluntary revivalist activities, they need not decline, and may even prosper in their new roles.

Under such conditions, Wilson's observation of a correlation between public activity and decline appears not to hold, and thus it seems that religion may play an important role in social integration and the promotion of civility in highly differentiated societies, contrary to Seligman's prognosis. However, it is important to note that for Casanova the 'caesaropapist' path of a close alliance with the state, attempting to control the public sphere, does lead to decline. Our argument has placed substantial weight on Casanova's claims, and therefore the next section will subject these to further scrutiny, locating his Polish and Brazilian examples in a broader context.

## Christianity and civil society in Central and Eastern Europe and Latin America

In Central and Eastern Europe (CEE) there is strong evidence that religion contributed to the process of democratic transition, despite its relative neglect as a factor by mainstream theorists (for example, Potter *et al.*, 1997). This contribution appears to have been made in four main ways. First, religion provided an institutional space in otherwise totalitarian societies, within which it was possible to organize various forms of opposition to the communist state, as with Lutheran churches in East Germany (Cantrell and Kemp, 1993). Second, religion provided a symbolic resource, or fund of collective memories, which were mobilized to oppose or subvert state-imposed communist ideologies, as with the impact of Catholicism on the symbols and imagery of Solidarity in Poland (Kubik, 1994).

Third, religion functioned as an institutional and ideological connection with an international order which stretched beyond both the state and the communist bloc, as in Germany where links between Lutheran churches East and West persisted despite their organizational separation in 1968, and blossomed into peace movements on both sides of the iron curtain (De Gruchy, 1995: pp. 193–205). Fourth, religion functioned as an intellectual force from which opposition thinking and identities could be self-consciously constructed, for example the influence of Catholic intellectuals on opposition thinking in Poland, and on the members of Charter 77 in Czechoslovakia (Luxmoore and Babiuch, 1995a; 1995b).

However, churches have been less successful in the following period, either in sustaining high levels of mobilization or in supporting democratic consolidation. The East German case provides a strong counter-example to any general thesis of CEE religious revival, as falling membership and attendance have continued the established post-war pattern, and citizens' movements increasingly organized independently of the churches once public space opened up (Pollack, 1995: pp. 103–4).

But even here, the fact that the church provided space for public mobilization – in contrast to large variety of other intermediate organizations (Therborn, 1997: p. 47) – requires explanation. Why the church, even a declining one in a highly secularized society? One possibility is that religion implies a perspective from which to judge the existing order, locally manifest in the Lutheran doctrine of the two kingdoms (Krusche, 1994). Thus the church was the one institution that the party was unable to absorb ideologically. Furthermore, it would seem that such a perspective is implicit in all religious faith, according to Cantwell Smith's definition of faith as the insight that 'one lives in a world whose greatness transcends one grasp, but does not totally elude one' (1998: p. 130).

However, returning to the post-Communist period, it is not only in the former East Germany that churches have struggled to find a role. Even in Poland, where the identification of the Catholic Church with national identity is strong, and participation in worship high, attempts by the Church to put itself above democracy on issues including abortion, education and the constitution, have damaged its public support (Gilarek, 1997). Thus it would seem that where the churches identify with democracy under repressive conditions they have considerable ability to mobilize the public in support of democratic transformation. But under conditions of pluralization following democratic transition their mobilization capacity diminishes, especially where religion is not strongly associated with national identity on account of historic divisions (Germany, Czech Republic). Furthermore, where the church is strongly identified with the nation (Poland, many Orthodox countries) it is likely to be ambivalent in its support for democratic consolidation, because acceptance that its voice is only one among others may involve a perceived loss of authority. This may backfire, as in Poland; or it may increase the church's popularity where national identity is heightened by continuing ethnic tensions, as in Serbia and Russia.

Similar patterns may be observed in Latin America in opposition to right-wing oppression. Here, movements inspired by liberation theology (especially 'CEBs', 'base ecclesiastical communities') achieved high levels of public mobilization in opposition to military national security governments from the 1970s through to the mid-1980s, notably in Brazil and Nicaragua. As Casanova states of Brazil, 'In the 1970s ... a new Brazilian church emerged, the People's Church, which not only became the main force of opposition to the bureaucratic-authoritarian regime, supporting the reconstitution of civil society against the state, but also began to sponsor the radical transformation of Brazilian society' (1994: p. 118).

However, in both cases, after the initial successes of the 1979 revolution in Nicaragua and restoration of democracy in Brazil in 1985, the movements showed signs of decline (Kee, 1990; Nagle, 1997). This 'failure' appears to relate to several areas of 'performance': loss of religious distinctiveness caused by absorption of activists into the political mainstream, limited impact on the economic conditions of the poor, failure to mobilize the poorest sections of society, and dependence on a simplistic version of Marxism, with critics arguing both that movements were not rigorously Marxist enough (Kee, 1990), and that Marxist-derived dependency theory is inadequate to address the impact of the global economy (Beyer, 1994).

But the failure of the movement to address the residual economic problems of the global economy is not necessarily crucial to its political role in civil society, except where failure to deliver on promises may undermine its general credibility. Assessing the legacy of the movement, Levine comments (1999: p. 59):

> Core liberationist ideas have made their way into the mainstream. Among these are the salience of human rights, basic beliefs about participation, and the value accorded to active citizens in an independent society. A century from now, those looking back will surely locate the legacy of liberation theology in this broad effort to change the agenda of public discourse, and to make a legitimate place for active citizens in a more independent civil society.

This suggests that use of the term 'failure' to describe the impact of these movements needs qualification. Both the Eastern European and Latin American cases suggest that faith organizations have a substantial capacity to generate mobilization against an oppressive state. Indeed, one may concur with Mestrovic that Catholicism, once aligned with democracy and human rights following Vatican II, is particularly suited to this role, given its capacity to 'preserve culture, community and non-utilitarian individualism' (1993: p. 109). However, once democratic transition has occurred this mobilization capacity tends to diminish as the church, like other opposition movements, fragments into diverse interest groups. Religious groups which have identified almost wholly with secular goals may experience the sharpest decline under these conditions, as their rationale for independent existence is undermined. Yet this problem may apply less to liberation theology inspired movements than is sometimes thought, if Levine is correct in arguing that these always focused more on spiritual renewal than popular perceptions suggest (1999: p. 19). Furthermore, religious groups have taken on an important new civil society role as mediators in a number of post-transition truth commissions, in El Salvador, Chile, Brazil and Argentina (Levine 1999: p. 31), as well as South Africa. Additionally, the high levels of activity of women in these movements, in spite of their relative neglect at an intellectual level, suggests a further role in social transformation (ibid.).

## Conclusion

In making analytic use of the concept of civil society, the discussion in this chapter attempted to bracket assumptions about its democratizing influence, relationship with the state, and ethos; leaving a concept of intermediary organizations with some degree of autonomy, situated between family and state. The examples of faith organizations considered here suggests that these can contribute to the development of civility and trust in late/postmodern societies; though no longer through the vertical legitimizing relationship through which faith traditionally produced social cohesion, but rather through the network of horizontal relationships which faith communities may nurture both within themselves and with other groups. It was further suggested that these processes may be elucidated through a sociological reading of virtue ethics. Conservative religious traditions can play an important role here, without necessarily liberalizing themselves – as examples from contexts as diverse as Turkey, Bosnia and Britain suggest.

This positive thesis has been emphasized so as to counter prevalent assumptions concerning the virtue of secularism within theories of civil society. However a balanced picture must also recognize that where there is a strong association between religion, ethnicity and national identity (as in much of Eastern Europe, and in Northern Ireland), and in the absence of the internal reform of religious tradition (compare Catholicism and Orthodoxy), religion can also contribute to the *breakdown* of civility. Furthermore, the religious forces which might promote civility, participation and social cohesion, need to be considered in interaction with other factors. These include a range of cultural influences, economic and political variables – perhaps especially the extremes of economic inequality which militate against social cohesion, as we noted following Castells. Finally, and at a most general level, this brief survey of relations between faith, trust and civil society suggest that it is important to relocate the sociology and politics of religion back into the social scientific mainstream, and not to assume their irrelevance – whether due to an unreflective secular ideology, or to an inadequately formulated version of the secularization thesis.

# 4
# Trust, Social Capital and Economy

*Fran Tonkiss*

## Introduction

Debates over the nature and uses of 'trust' return to some very enduring concerns within social theory – problems of social order, the anatomy of civil society, the relation between individual and collective action. An interest in such questions represents more than simply the rehearsal of familiar themes; rather it marks a renewed argument for the relevance of *social* explanation in a range of fields, from education and health to urban development and governance. This social turn has been particularly striking in relation to economic issues. Here, perspectives on trust are central to accounts of 'social capital' that provide a critical counterpoint to dominant neoclassical models, by arguing for the effectiveness of social factors in shaping economic arrangements and outcomes.

The concept of 'social capital' has different origins, and its recent applications are even more diverse. From comparative development to theories of ethnic enterprise, studies of health and education to diagnoses of social exclusion, issues of urban regeneration to the economics of transition, the remit of social capital has become rather extended. As a theory of everything, social capital can end up explaining rather little – especially when it functions simply as a quasi-technical proxy for talking about 'the social'. The discussion in this chapter is concerned with issues of trust and social capital in a more narrowly economic sense. It begins by looking briefly at the relation of the economy to notions of civil society, before turning to the category of social capital as a means of accounting for the social features of economic action. The constituent notions of trust, norms and networks are traced to key influences within the new economic sociology and new institutional economics – with the suggestion that these should be treated as economic categories, rather than as social factors that somehow are prior to economic interactions. The latter part of the discussion examines recent applications of social capital to the analysis of comparative economic performance and economic development, arguing for an emphasis on the role of wider social conditions – and especially structures of inequality – on determining the effectiveness of local forms of social capital.

## Economy and civil society

The economy has played a variable role within theories of civil society. A chief concern within this broad tradition of thought (for such different thinkers as Hobbes, Locke, Rousseau, Hegel, Paine or Tocqueville), has been with the form and limits of political authority: a problem which came to be posed in terms of a distinction between civil society and the state (see Tonkiss, 1998). If civil society has schematically been defined in contrast to the state, on the one hand, and the 'private' realm of the family, on the other, its relation to the economy has been less clear. In certain versions the civil sphere includes market exchange and institutions; in others, the latter stand outside it, sometimes in a hostile relation. Locke's conception of the civil realm was founded on natural rights of property; and the economic dimensions of civil association were especially pronounced in the works of Scottish Enlightenment thinkers such as Ferguson and Smith. Adam Ferguson pointed to the emphasis, within philosophies of civil society, on calculations of individual interest and the pursuit of commerce (Ferguson, 1782: Section I, III); while Adam Smith clearly identified civil society with the sphere of private exchange. A similar economic conception is central to Marx's early critique of bourgeois civil society (Marx, 1970; 1977). However later Marxian approaches – in particular the influential account of Gramsci, and Habermas' treatment of the 'life-world' – differentiate a civil sphere from both state *and* economy (see Keane, 1998: pp. 15–18).

Normative models of civil society tend to bracket out economic relations, focusing instead on those forms of association – clubs, societies, religious and voluntary organizations, charities, community groups, campaigning movements – whose rationale might be seen as more 'civic' than economic in character (see Cohen and Arato, 1992; Powell and Guerin, 1997). The perspective of a Paine or Tocqueville, as it were, would seem to take precedence over that of a Ferguson or Smith. At the same time, however, something of a consensus recently has emerged on the importance of a 'healthy' civil society for the development of effective economic institutions – a point, as Fukuyama has it, on which 'virtually all serious observers' now agree (Fukuyama, 1996: p. 4). Indeed, in his study of civic traditions in Italy, Putnam argues that levels of 'civic engagement' within regions can help to explain – and even to predict – levels of economic development (Putnam, 1993a: pp. 152–62).

A key impetus for this recent interest in the links between economy and civil society has been the difficult path of post-Communist transition. The experience of post-Communist economies in Central and Eastern Europe – and that of Russia in particular – puts into question any easy linkage of free markets to economic efficiency and prosperity. Intense speculation twinned with powerful capitalist ideology meant that the challenges facing these transitional economies at times were reduced to a crude choice between unfettered markets and a reversion to communism. However deregulation and privatization could not in themselves ensure economic efficiency, let alone political stability or social welfare. The 'shock therapy' introduction of economic liberalism in contexts, such as Russia or Poland, that had no existing traditions of political or civic liberalism, failed to provide the conditions for an effective *market culture*. While the informal economy marked out a limited market sphere under communism, this was vulnerable to forms of exploitation, corruption and menace that work to reduce the efficiency of economic exchanges. Indeed, the logic of the informal economy can be seen as hostile to free market relations – as cronyism, racketeering and mistrust undermine effects of liberalization – as much as it is hostile to the regulation of markets through legal and policy measures. One explanation for Russia's problems of transition is the way that behaviour in the informal economy provided a model for conduct in the post-Communist market: corruption had become so commonplace by the end of the 1990s as to make honest market behaviour an irrational economic choice.

Russia's problems, in particular, seem to support an argument that norms of social exchange and market conduct – and generalized resources of trust – are crucial to economic efficiency. Several theorists have argued that the weakness of civil society was a critical factor in Russia's flawed transition (see Crawford, 1995; Przeworski, 1991; Woolcock, 1998). The fact that state socialism had suppressed those unofficial forms of association characteristic of a liberal civil society hindered the shift to a market-style economy, and the development of the complex networks of trust that underpin economic as well as social exchange (see Sztompka, 1998b). In an extended sense, it might be argued that 'markets' had stood as a proxy for 'freedom' in the collapse of communism, in the absence of any fully realized notion of civic freedoms in an associational sphere (see Habermas, 1990).

These perspectives intersect with theories of social capital in linking economic action to a more general concept of associational life. In so doing, they displace conventional distinctions between 'economy' and 'civil society' as discrete (sometimes hostile) spheres. If social capital, however, offers a way of resolving the boundary question in respect of economy and civil society, the conceptual limits of this term are not themselves always clear.

## Accounting for social capital

Accounting for social capital is hardly an exact science. Definitions proliferate within the theoretical literature, and researchers have operationalized the concept in several ways (see, for example, Putnam, 1995b; Putnam *et al.*, 2000; Halpern, 1998). Woolcock glosses various uses of the term as broadly referring to 'the information, trust, and norms of reciprocity inhering in one's social networks' (Woolcock, 1998: p. 153); while Putnam takes it to indicate those 'features of social organization, such as trust, norms, and networks, that can improve the efficiency of society by facilitating co-ordinated actions' (Putnam, 1993a: p. 167).

Claims regarding the pedigree of the term provide a diverting sideline to the larger debate (see Woolcock, 1998: p. 192n). A common early point of reference is the statement by Jane Jacobs in her classic work on *The Death and Life of the Great American Cities*: '[N]etworks are a city's irreplaceable social capital. Whenever the capital is lost, from whatever cause, the income from it disappears, never to return until and unless new capital is slowly and chancily accumulated' (Jacobs, 1961: p. 138).

Jacobs, clearly, is using the notion of social capital as a metaphor. However, social scientists more recently have tried to specify this form of 'capital' with greater precision, to make it more directly comparable to other kinds of economic capital, and to render it measurable (see Knack and Keefer, 1995; Uslaner, 1997; Whiteley, 1997; Halpern, 1998; cf. Baron and Hannon, 1994).

Social capital is analagous to forms of physical, financial and human capital, in that it facilitates economic processes and helps to command economic resources. It also has distinguishing features.[1] First, social capital – as a property of groups or networks – has a collective rather than an individual character. While social capital can be exploited by individuals (when someone uses their personal networks to get a job, for example), this form of capital is not independently *held* by the individual. It is not, in this sense, so easily transferable as financial capital, or as mobile as human capital. Second (and in common with human capital) it tends to be enhanced, rather than diminished, by use. When people work together to realize a collective aim, they frequently consolidate their 'stocks' of social capital. Of course, this is not always the case: groups efforts can be successful in terms of instrumental outcomes while beset by acrimony and disappointment; but teamwork also can become more effective the more often it is undertaken. Third, while social capital is 'slowly and chancily' generated over time (Jacobs, 1961: p. 138), it can quickly be lost. One bad apple or bad mistake can seriously undermine collective resources of trust and weaken social ties. Finally, elements of social capital such as trust and co-operative relations are viewed as having intrinsic value, quite apart from their capacity to facilitate economic outcomes. This 'moral' dimension of social capital is problematic in several respects. In a primary analytic sense, a moralized version of social capital can appear as an end in itself, obscuring the ways in which social resources are capitalized by different actors.

There are important precedents for a more instrumental definition of social capital. Pierre Bourdieu developed the concept in the 1970s to refer to the benefits and resources that accrue from membership of certain social networks, with particular reference to issues of education and cultural reproduction (see Bourdieu and Passeron, 1990 [1970]; Bourdieu and Wacquant, 1992). Bourdieu's work is concerned with the way that social capital links with economic and other forms of capital in reproducing social advantages and inequalities (see Bourdieu, 1986). James Coleman also used the case of education (in this instance, comparative rates of high school dropout) in his highly influential essay on the role of social capital in fostering human capital (Coleman, 1988). If Coleman's work has been overtaken by more recent developments in the field, the basis of his claims for the value of social capital as a 'conceptual tool' (ibid.: S96) remains highly relevant to the present discussion. Coleman's argument is directed towards the rational action paradigm that is central to neoclassical accounts of economic behaviour, and informs rational choice approaches in related disciplines such as sociology, psychology and political science. In this context, his use of social capital forms part of a larger theoretical project to bring together models of rational action with an analysis of social structure – to effect, that is, a kind of *rapprochement* between economics and sociology (see Coleman, 1987; 1990).

Coleman's definition of social capital is rather opaque. All forms of social capital, he contends, 'consist of some aspect of social structures, and they facilitate certain actions of actors – whether persons or corporate actors – within the structure' (Coleman, 1988: S98). Social capital is *productive*, he goes on, in that it enables actions or outcomes that would not be possible (or would not occur so easily) without it. His meaning is made clearer by way of examples from a number of economic and non-economic contexts – the wholesale diamond market in New York, clandestine study circles among South Korean student activists, the relative safety for children of public parks in Jerusalem, the Kahn El Khalili market in Cairo – where social networks, interpersonal trust, cultural norms and informal sanctions work to facilitate and regulate social action and economic exchange.

The notion of social capital, then, 'calls out' various elements of social structure in terms of the function these serve in enabling actors to achieve particular ends. Rather than providing a mute backdrop to members' economic activities – let alone an 'irrational' sphere of traditional and affective ties – the close cultural, religious and family networks of Jewish diamond-traders in Brooklyn (to pursue Coleman's much-cited example) provide effective 'security' for their exchanges, and obviate the need for costly and complex forms of contract and insurance. As Coleman admits, social capital in itself remains something of an 'unanalysed concept' (ibid.: S101); however it directs analytic attention to the way that aspects of social organization provide resources for purposive action.

Coleman's account hinges upon a stylized distinction between structure and agency as frameworks for understanding human behaviour, and his notion of social capital is primarily a means of socializing the rational action paradigm to which he generally adheres. More recent approaches to social capital deal less in the language of social structure, than in that of social networks. None the less, Coleman's account outlines key forms of social capital that have been prominent in a range of later definitions:

(i) 'obligations and expectations' – what elsewhere figures as norms of reciprocity or trust;
(ii) 'information channels' – or social networks;
(iii) 'norms and effective sanctions' – including systems of shared values (Coleman, 1988: S102–S105; cf. Fukuyama, 1996; Putnam, 1993a).

In this sense, Coleman takes various forms of social capital as analytically separate. Other approaches to social capital – in particular Robert Putnam's – have been criticized for treating trust, norms and networks in an undifferentiated way that blunts the conceptual salience of each term (see Newton, 1997; Anheier and Kendall, 1998). There is a danger that the different forms disappear into a catch-all notion of social capital that does little to explain how each or any of them work, in particular contexts, to facilitate specific ends.

## Trust and social capital

Trust regularly features – together with norms and networks – within definitions of social capital (Putnam, 1993a: p. 167; 1995a: p. 67; 1995b: pp. 664–5; Fukuyama, 1996: p. 26; Woolcock, 1998: p. 153). However, the meaning of trust itself can be hard to grasp. Other theorists note the difficulty of defining trust, and point to the different senses in which it variously is used (Seligman, 1997: pp. 17–26; cf. Luhmann, 1988; Giddens, 1994). Fukuyama is notable, among theorists of social capital, in essaying a definition: trust, for him, refers to 'the expectation that arises within a community of regular, honest and cooperative behaviour, based on commonly shared norms' (Fukuyama, 1996: p. 26). He sees trust not simply as a *component* or *indicator* of social capital, but as its precondition: 'social capital is a capability that arises from the prevalence of trust in a society or in certain parts of it' (ibid.). Fukuyama's usage does not always appear consistent (sometimes he seems to conflate trust with social capital, for example, or to use the terms interchangeably); but then, trust is a hard term to pin down. Certainly, there are different levels of abstraction at work in these debates: for Fukuyama, trust represents an underlying form of social solidarity, as well as a specific relation; for others, trust is treated more simply as a component (if a necessary one) of social capital (see Putnam, 1993a: p. 170; 1995a; 1995b; Halpern, 1998). Invariably however, trust is something that can be thought about, and measured, in terms of 'levels': whether in Fukuyama's schematic distinction between 'high-trust' and 'low-trust' societies; through quantitative surveys of public trust (see Putnam, 1995b; Putnam *et al.*, 2000); or, as tends to be the case in the development literature, on the basis of ethnographic or anecdotal evidence (see Woolcock, 1998: pp. 152–3, 173, 203 n.104; see also Hart, 1988).

A basic analytic problem in taking trust as a component of social capital is the weight of moral baggage that the term carries with it. This is perhaps hard to avoid, given the resonance of 'trust' as a moral category in different – especially personal – contexts. Notions of social capital tend to run together ethical and economic conceptions of trust. On one side, trust represents a social good; on the other side, its use within theories of social capital bears a family resemblance to conventional economic definitions of trust. Social trust can be seen as an end in itself, as well as a 'lubricant' or resource for action (see Luhmann, 1988). Social networks, in contrast, may be good things to have (depending on what you can get out of them), but do not necessarily represent a public good as such. Woolcock points out the confusion this creates as to whether social capital, understood in terms of networks and ties, refers to the structure of social relations, or understood in terms of trust, to their

– of particular forms of social capital is a local and a critical question, rather than an analytic assumption. Where an entrepreneur draws on family networks to finance a business start-up that both creates jobs and provides a local service, their use of social capital is both effective and broadly beneficial. Where personal ties are used to restrict jobs to an ethnic in-group – as in the control by white minorities over New York construction trades, or the nepotism that long excluded black employees from working as drivers at Ford in England – social capital is instrumentally effective, but linked to racism, discrimination and exclusion (see Portes and Landolt, 1996; see also Loury, 1987).

Approaches to social capital can be problematic in taking as given, factors – such as trust, norms and networks – that themselves require definition in specific contexts. A greater problem is the tendency of social capital as an analytic device to slide into a moral category. In this connection, it is instructive to look to alternative accounts that offer analysis of the 'social' features of 'economic' action, while suppressing some of the normative 'noise' that surrounds notions of social capital.

## Trust, norms and networks: antecedents of social capital

Two key antecedents for theories of social capital are to be found in the fields of sociology and economics – respectively, in new economy sociology and in institutional economics. In asserting the relevance of social factors and explanations, approaches to social capital are a critical challenge to the sway of neoclassical economics – particularly given the latter's influence upon neo-liberal policy since the 1970s. In this way, debates regarding social capital re-visit the disciplinary disputes that have marked out economics and sociology as distinct intellectual fields. A conventional division of intellectual labour is captured in the economist Paul Samuelson's claim that it is possible to 'separate economics from sociology upon the basis of rational and irrational behaviour', where rationality was understood in terms of an economic theory of utility (Samuelson, 1955: p. 90). While economists concerned themselves with rational, maximizing behaviour as typified by market actors, sociology was taken up with formally irrational (affective, rule-governed, customary, deviant, group) behaviour. This nice distinction served to distinguish a formal model of economic exchange from an extended sphere of social interaction.

The new economic sociology that came to prominence in the 1980s, however, puts into question an analytic separation of 'economic' from more general processes of 'social' exchange (see Swedberg, 1991; Granovetter and Swedberg, 1992; Smelser and Swedberg, 1994). Economic models, it was argued, had the effect of abstracting – or 'disembedding' – economic action from its social context (Granovetter, 1985; cf. Polanyi, 1992). Rather than viewing economic relations in terms of atomized exchange, the former were bound up in economic and non-economic networks and institutions (Polanyi, 1992: p. 34). The concept of networks is at the heart of the new economic sociology, as these work to structure economic flows: 'economic institutions are constructed by mobilization of resources through social networks' (Granovetter and Sweberg, 1992: p. 18). In turn, economic institutions – from firms to trade associations to market-stalls – create and reproduce social networks.

Recent theories of social capital have a further precedent in the 'new institutional economics' associated with the work of Ronald Coase and his followers (see Coase, 1937; 1960; 1984; Williamson, 1975; 1985). This perspective on institutions is based on the idea that there are 'social costs' involved in economic transactions – in particular, the time and money cost of searching for information in markets, and the cost of securing contracts. Firms reduce their social costs by capturing information in the form of their workforce's expertise. Williamson (1985) extends this analysis, examining how hierarchical and network structures each can be used to minimize transaction costs: either by co-ordinating functions internally (in hierarchical firms) or by maintaining relational contracts (in stable networks) that avoid the necessity of frequent one-off exchanges with many, in principle unknown, external actors.

Coase and Williamson remain firmly within a neoclassical framework, explaining economic institutions in terms of how these maximize efficiency. What is more, they conceive of instititutions as *formal* mechanisms for reducing social costs and securing information. Alternative strands of institutional economics, in contrast, use an extended definition of 'institutions' to refer not simply to formal structures but also to the routines, rules and norms that order economic action and exchange (see North, 1990; Hodgson,

1994). In this conception, economic actors draw on explicit *and* implicit rules to orient their own behaviour, and tacitly expect others to follow them also. It is shared norms and expectations, then – as well as more formal or legal rules – that guide economic action. Moreover, personal ties and informal networks work in tandem with relational contracts in co-ordinating economic exchanges. This understanding is consonant with that of an economic sociologist such as Granovetter, who argues that both formal and informal relations shape economic processes, including relations within and between firms (Granovetter, 1985).

These perspectives have particular implications for thinking about trust as an economic relation. If firms or contracts can be viewed as *formal* mechanisms for reducing uncertainty in economic transactions, 'trust' provides a category for analysing the *informal* means of doing so. Trust, that is, refers to the mediation of economic risk by way of informal relations and rules. At the most basic level, it is a shared understanding of the rules of exchange that allows economic actors to hold expectations about others' behaviour, and to proceed – in the absence of perfect information or legal security – on the basis of a kind of 'trust'. This economic version of trust rests on assumptions about norms, and is built up through routinized exchanges. It is evident in Coleman's example of the New York diamond traders, whose social networks are productive of a kind of trust that is neither simply social nor strictly economic in character. Such a conception of trust also appears in anthropological literature on the emergence of market economies, particularly given the historical role of middlemen in mediating between buyers and sellers (Plattner, 1989; see also Seligman, 1997: pp. 81–2). These developing trading patterns depend on people's ability to form stable expectations about the economic behaviour of others, based on the iteration of market exchange. A form of 'trust', to take a further example, has been seen as a key element of transactions within financial markets, such as those in the City of London, that at one time were based on face-to-face interaction. The increased mediation of these capital markets by information technology has put such relations of trust – 'my word is my bond' – into question, although some research has noted attempts by international traders to socialize their on-line transactions in ways which mimic the 'trust' relations of face-to-face dealing (see Thrift, 1993; 1994).

Economic exchanges, then, are conditioned by particular contexts; are repeated over time; and linked into more or less formal networks. While Coleman's account of the diamond merchants stresses the social regulation of economic behaviour, processes of exchange also are shaped by economic norms that do not reduce either to social ties or legal sanctions. Such norms of economic conduct tend to discourage if not always prevent perfidy or opportunism – employees do not routinely embezzle their firms; people often (as the economists love to cite) leave tips in restaurants that they will never visit again. Probity and honesty, that is, are produced as positive economic values that allow individuals to form expectations about each other's behaviour, and which increase the efficiency of economic exchange.

Trust, norms and networks commonly are taken as the key elements of social capital, underpinning a range of economic relations and processes. It would be an error, however, to see these 'social' factors as somehow prior to economic action. Equally, they are *emergent within* economic exchanges. Perspectives drawn from new economic sociology and institutional economics do not support any easy separation of the 'social' from the 'economic'; nor do they establish the analytic priority of either term. This point goes beyond the truism that all economic relations are ultimately social in character, to focus on how specific economic arrangements are organized through mixes of personal ties, institutional networks, rules and norms of conduct.

## Social capital and economic performance

If it is now a commonplace of economic sociology that economic exchanges are embedded in social networks and norms, these arguments recently have been extended to the analysis of comparative growth. Fukuyama (1996) treats social capital – associational networks, collective values, cultural norms – as key determinants of macro-economic performance. He argues that certain 'arts of association', and the relations of trust on which they rest, underpin different societies' chances of economic success. The contention is that those societies whose members are given to 'spontaneous sociability' in the form of voluntary association (such as, under his definition, the United States or Japan) also tend to economic prosperity. Forms of intermediate association, from Lions Clubs to tea ceremonies, represent a network of 'moral communities' that 'generate the kind of social trust that is critical to organizational efficiency' in a broader (and an economic) sense (Fukuyama, 1996: p. 309). Neoclassical economic theory – despite its extended explanatory powers – is unable to grasp the economic importance of relationships that stand outside market exchange. In Fukuyama's account, therefore, mainstream economic theory must be supplemented by an analysis of economic cultures.

While Robert Putnam differs from Fukuyama in important respects (particularly concerning the role of the state in promoting social capital), he also has used a broad analysis of social capital to account for comparative economic performance. Most notably, he employs this concept to explain the success of industrial districts in the 'Third Italy', based upon a distinctive governance mix of competition and co-operation – or markets and networks – in research, design and innovation, factor markets, administration, warehousing, marketing and so on (see Putnam, 1993a). Putnam's account is heavily influenced by the insights of new institutional economics; although he places greater emphasis on the importance of networks in embedding social norms, as well as on their role in limiting transaction costs. The perspectives offered by political scientists such as Fukuyama and Putnam, furthermore, link up with recent arguments in the economics of comparative growth. Endogenous growth theory, as it gained influence over the 1990s, shifted attention to the effects of local social factors on rates of economic growth and development. Such an approach maintains that growth lags between nations and regions do not only reflect disparities in technical capacity or physical capital, but also differences in human capital – in resources of knowledge and skill. 'Ideas gaps', that is, are as important as 'object gaps' in explaining differential rates of growth (see Romer, 1993; 1994). If human capital provided the initial focus within theories of endogenous growth – and inspired a government penchant for supply-side economic strategies based on education and training (see Shaw, 1997) – an expanded notion of social capital was not far behind. The growing interest of the World Bank in the role of social capital in development contexts is only the most striking evidence of this trend.

It is interesting to observe how issues of social capital and endogenous growth (that mutually stress the local social determinants of economic success) have come to prominence against a backdrop of economic globalization. In this context, local social factors can confer a form of competitive advantage (or disadvantage), or more simply determine the forms of access to global markets. An intrinsic relation between 'the local' and 'the global' is now rather taken for granted within social theory; however the economic changes associated with globalization raise serious questions as to the 'sociality' of contemporary economic processes. The disaggregation of manufacturing industry, the decline of industrial towns and cities, the decrease in plant sizes; the dispersal of production processes across international space; increased labour 'flexibility' and insecurity; the increasing mediation of work by new technology – all point to a 'disembedding' of numerous people's economic lives from local or stable social networks. While forms of globalization or flexible accumulation are linked to the emergence of new industrial districts and to high-level professional and expert networks, they also mark the erosion of older or less elite patterns of concentration and conviviality, based on the embeddedness of firms and industries, proximity (and security) in the workplace and the labour process. Integration into 'global' networks is nice work, if you can get it; but the linkages that exemplify contemporary capitalist economies – intensified in time and extended over space – often occur at the cost of more local forms of social connectedness. In this context, approaches to social capital sit within a battery of supply-side economic strategies that aim to link localities into new economic networks.

## Uneven economies of social capital

Theorists such as Fukuyama and Putnam develop their accounts of social capital on a regional, even national, level – which would seem to involve rather large claims for the extended 'strength of weak ties' (cf. Granovetter, 1973). However, the greater part of the economic literature on social capital is more closely concerned with local questions of economic development. An important strand of work in this context derives from economic anthropology and development studies, especially in terms of how social networks can mediate or substitute for formal economic institutions (see Hart, 1988; Woolcock, 1998). A key interest here has been on the mobilization of financial and physical capital through local networks; as in micro-finance arrangements where group members become a mutual source of credit and collateral, or in networks of ethnic enterprise (see Rhodes and Nabi, 1992). In his influential early essay on the rotating credit association in a Javanese context, Clifford Geertz argues that this represents a very specific form of collective action, and one based on reckonings of mutual and individual interest rather than on any larger ethos of co-operation (Geertz, 1962). Such an analysis gainsays simple assumptions about the sociality of local development initiatives. Local finance arrangements can provide an effective means of commanding resources in the absence of reliable economic institutions, and can reproduce themselves as a more or less stable form of social capital – a developmental 'middle-rung' (Geertz, 1962) – located between social ties and formal institutions.

Such a perspective is important in directing attention to the effects of social capital; to the specific ways, that is, in which social and cultural relations facilitate economic outcomes. Forms of social capital are not simply or necessarily conducive to economic development, in two key respects. The first has to do with *inequality*, the second with questions of *capacity*. Where resources of social capital are unevenly distributed, social networks can be a basis for corruption, cronyism and other forms of rent-seeking behaviour (Woolcock, 1998: p. 163; see also Portes and Landolt, 1996). Certain in-groups or networks are able to command inequitable shares of public goods, to monopolize information, and to close off opportunities and access to others – whether in terms of the benefits accruing to party apparatchiks or government officials; in the form of insider dealing; or the way in which sections of the middle classes tend to enjoy greater access to welfare state services (see Bryson, 1992).

These arguments shift the 'moral dimensions' of social capital away from the value of networks, trust and norms as goods in themselves, to a critical take on the way these are shaped, sustained and closed off by wider social conditions. As Woolcock (1998) points out, poverty, inequality, discrimination, economic and political instability, authoritarian or weak government all militate against the effective formation and mobilization of social capital, and against economic development in a larger sense. Taking these factors into account is important if one wishes to avoid narrowly economistic or culturalist explanations of economic 'backwardness'.

These points open on to questions of *capacity* in relation to networks of social capital. The fact of possessing social ties, that is, does not guarantee that these connections will help you to command other resources. Social networks cannot simply *create* physical or financial capital where this does not already exist. Fukuyama, for example, explains the economic disadvantage of African-American populations in terms of deficits of social capital, particularly in the form of social trust. In this context, he posits a 'causal linkage between inability to cohere socially and poverty' (Fukuyama, 1996: p. 303). Quite apart from the deep culturalist assumptions underlying this argument, Fukuyama views questions of social capital (the 'inability to cohere socially') as causally *prior* to questions of economic capital (poverty). Such a construction falls prey to a kind of 'deficit theory syndrome' (see Morrow, 1999), where social capital becomes something that disadvantaged individuals and communities lack, and which in a circular way comes to *explain* their disadvantage (see also Portes and Landolt, 1996). In contrast to Fukuyama, Wilson (1996) has argued – also in a US context – that many impoverished areas and populations have strong social ties, but are isolated from 'mainstream' economic and social networks. 'Network poverty' in this sense refers not to the absence or weakness of social networks, but to the difficulty of accessing opportunities or resources through these networks. Talk about 'social capital', here, can become a way of not talking about poverty.

## Conclusion

Perspectives on trust and social capital offer ways of reinstating social factors within economic analysis. In an economic context, however, it is important to separate out a moral discourse of social capital as a value in itself, from the instrumental effectiveness of trust, norms and networks in securing certain economic outcomes. A more critical perspective on social capital, then, might look to the way that wider social factors shape the efficacy of social capital among different groups. Inequity, discrimination, insecurity and poverty can inhibit the development of social capital, but can also negate its effects. Viewing social capital in terms of *capacity*, then, allows one to focus on the way that social networks and resources of trust can be *capitalized* as resources for economic action.

## Note

1. The discussion here draws on Woolcock (1998: pp. 191–2, n.11).

# 5
# State, Welfare and Civil Society
*Fred Powell*

## Introduction

The term 'civil society' has in recent years enjoyed something of a revival. Politicians and academics in many countries have embraced it as a prescriptive model for the future organization of society. Exponents of civil society present it as a mediating space between the private and public spheres in a pluralist democracy. As Wedel has put it, 'a civil society exists when individuals and groups are free to form organizations that function independently and that can mediate between citizens and the state' (Wedel, 1994: p. 323). Amid widespread political disillusionment with the welfare state and its capacity to solve social problems, calls for the reinvigoration of civil society have gained ground.

Civil society is frequently equated with the voluntary or non-governmental sector. However, there is a case for broadening this conception of civil society to embrace a wider consideration of the meaning of citizenship in contemporary society, and the moral economy of the welfare state in an era when fiscal and social conservatism has once again become dominant; as evident in demands for a return to basic 'family values' and for welfare reform. While perspectives on civil society most typically have seen this sphere as distinct from that of the family, the latter has come to feature in arguments for civic and social renewal. Social conservatives long have emphasized the civic role of the family; more recently, theorists of new social democratic forms have contended that 'the family is a basic institution of civil society' (Giddens, 1998: p. 89). Certainly, much of the debate about welfare reform in advanced liberal democracies has devolved on to the family, as a site where the duties of the state and the claims of the social, the obligations of the public and the responsibilities of the private, are negotiated and played out.

This chapter begins by examining the meaning of society and individualism in an era of 'postmodernity'. It goes on to consider how notions of social capital and civic voluntarism might be seen as displacing more welfarist approaches to collective well-being, and concludes by analysing the changing nature of family welfare in an era when trust has become a defining paradigm. At the centre of the discussion is an analysis of 'civil society' as a concept that, viewed from different perspectives, has 'the capacity for making sense of such disparate phenomena as the resistance to totalitarianism, the rise of neo-conservatism, the growth of social movements and the future of the welfare state' (Keane, 1988b: p. 2). Just as a broad notion of civil society was called upon to help interpret the major political shifts of the late twentieth century, so it has been harnessed to programmes for a 'new' kind of politics in the next. Giddens has declared that 'the fostering of an active civil society is a basic part of the politics of the third way' (Giddens, 1998: p. 78). A major problem with the 'politics of the third way', however, is its lack of a worked-out alternative vision that clearly differentiates it from the politics of neo-conservatism – a weakness Giddens (1998: pp. 77–8) frankly acknowledges: 'the new democratic state is an ideal, and something of an open-ended one at that. I don't pretend to unpack any of the detail that would be needed to give it real flesh'. The relationship between democratic state forms and an 'active civil society', however, is neither self-evident nor straightforward. If civil movements in Eastern Europe provided much of the impetus for a revival of interest in concepts of civil society in the 1980s (see Keane, 1988b), the experience of post-Communist transition puts into question any easy linkage of civil society with political democracy.

## Postmodernity, society and individualism

Postmodern societies might be defined in terms of risk, polarization, global markets, chronic change and fragmentation. As Stokes and Knight (1997) have observed, 'today we seem to be plunging into a chaotic, privatised future, recapturing medieval extremes of wealth and squalor'. As Gray (1998) puts it, 'when trust becomes a central category in social theory and political discourse it is a sign that something has been lost' (*Times Literary Supplement*, 27 May 1998). But just *what* has been lost is a vexed question, given that trust is itself a problematic construct.

On the face of it, postmodern societies are both atomized and fractured. Yet there is a paradox at work that confounds such conclusions. While the self, in the form of the independent citizen, may have become sovereign in their choice of lifestyles, solidarity is maintained by recognition-based social relations such as love, friendship, trust, empathy and compassion, charity, altruism, mutualism and the willingness to make sacrifices for others. In short, as Berking observes, 'these are cognitive, normative and emotional competencies which anything but reduce interest in the other to a mode of merely strategic interaction' (Berking, 1996: p. 192). Love and friendship most clearly belong to the private sphere. Charity, altruism and mutualism operate in the space between government and market occupied by the 'voluntary' or 'third sector'. These virtues point towards the continued existence of active citizenship in the form of participation, and dutiful citizenship in the form of obligation towards others. Trust, empathy and compassion are the common elements that transcend utilitarian individualism and define a form of 'solidary individualism' (Berking, 1996). This is an essential contradiction within contemporary Western societies, and one around which forms of civic trust might be mobilized in the context of an increasingly fragmented and polarized social order.

Berking observes that 'the triumphant advance of utilitarian values, which now seem to oblige the individual to secure and augment his own advantage, is today described under the heading detraditionalisation and individualisation, above all the cumulative effect of the process of cultural modernisation' (Berking, 1996: p. 191).

Yet the assumption that the modern individual is less committed to the other than his or her traditional counterpart is doubtful. Indeed, Carmen (1990: p. 4) argues that the reverse is the case:

> Traditional society is essentially non-participant. It deploys people by kinship into communities isolated by each other and from the centre. Modernity, on the other hand, is essentially a

mode of communication and participation. What makes communication possible, the sociological pivot upon which hinges the activation of psychic mobility, is the acquisition of literacy. An increase in literacy and therefore an increase in the capacity to empathise is the very yeast which permeates the system of self-sustaining growth and mass consumption. This is the ne plus ultra of modernity and by implication of development. Empathy is the bridge, which makes transition from traditional to modern ways feasible.

Other commentators who have sought to examine the nature and quality of trust, and its connections with both co-operation and prosperity, have also suggested a positive correlation between structures of 'modernity' and social connectedness (Fukuyama, 1996: Putnam, 1993a). Fukuyama argued that developed societies such as the USA, Germany and Japan were all 'high-trust' societies compared with less developed societies, such as Latin Catholic countries and China which, he concluded, were 'low-trust' societies. Similarly, in Italy Putnam found higher levels of civic trust in the more developed northern region, 'Padania', than in the less developed south. We might conclude that, despite tendencies towards fragmentation and polarization, modern forms of social organization potentially engender social participation and more sophisticated forms of communication between people that in turn promote empathy and trust.

This represents a central paradox in analysing contemporary social forms. On the face of it, such an analysis produces a two-world theory of an economic world defined by utilitarian values and a social world defined by solidaristic values. However, Fukuyama (1996) and Putnam (1993a) contend that trust and solidaristic values in the social sphere are positively correlated with the creation of prosperity in the economic sphere. In effect, they claim to have discovered a civilizational configuration between altruism and self-interest. However, it should be noted that the three fastest growing post-war economies were Japan, France and Italy – one 'high-trust' and two 'low-trust' societies by Fukuyama's reckoning. A more realistic assessment of the Fukuyama and Putnam theses is that these represent a reconfiguration of 'the social' in an era when neo-conservatism and global capital have become dominant and 'the social' increasingly fragmented and privatized. In this context, Fukuyama's characterization of the United States as a typically 'high-trust' society would appear to be confounded by such diverse factors as the high levels of incarceration and the legal regulation of personal life (as, for example, in prenuptial contracts).

For neo-conservatives, there is no substantive 'society', only individual enterprise and self-reliance. Hayek has contended that 'the social' is merely 'something which has developed as a practice of individual action in the course of social evolution' (Hayek, 1976: p. 78). For Hayek, 'the social' was an abhorrent concept that conjured up images of totalitarianism – in *The Mirage of Social Justice* (1976), he equates the pursuit of equality with tyranny. Conservative social theorists have challenged notions of social solidarity as a normative basis for the welfare systems which they view as creating a dependent 'underclass' (Gilder, 1981; Murray, 1984; Marsland, 1995; 1996). Marsland (1995: p. 4) has likened welfare to a 'cancer in the body politic' and added that 'it has also spread its contagion through more and more organs of society'. He concluded that 'only markets can provide effectively for the range and ambition of human wants and needs (Marsland, 1996: p. 140).

Neo-conservative politicians have taken the debate into the public arena, attacking social solidarity as the embodiment of collectivism. In their zealous efforts to destroy collectivism, they have sought to deny the existence of the social, most literally in Margaret Thatcher's famous aphorism – 'there is no such thing as society' (*The Sunday Times*, 9 November 1988). Thatcher then went on to elaborate her ideas in a controversial speech to the Assembly of the Church of Scotland in which she asserted that it was, above all, within the family that the 'the nursery of civic virtue' lay. She contended that the family was the basis on which governments should construct their policies for 'welfare, education and care' (Thatcher, quoted in Squires, 1990: p. 5). Neo-conservatism has, therefore, sought to write the obituary of 'the social' and looked backwards nostalgically to Burkean or Tocquevillian visions of smaller units of social responsibility, notably the family and the community. The denial of 'the social' is, consequently, not a denial of social responsibility. It simply means that the social rights of the entitled citizen of the welfare state are replaced by the social obligations of the dutiful citizen, in a reconstituted order where the market replaces society as the arbiter of moral values.

Teeple (1995: pp. 150–1) has characterized the much-vaunted triumph of neo-conservatism and the global market as the coming 'tyranny', observing that:

> Capitalism must increasingly confront the world that it has made, the results of its own expansion: seriously degraded nature; an increasingly impoverished working class; growing political autocracy and declining legitimacy, and new forms of resistance. Here, largely unfettered by political considerations, is a tyranny unfolding – an economic regime of unaccountable rules, a totalitarianism not of the political but of the economic.

Other commentators have taken a more optimistic view, detecting a new social complexity in which a more democratic citizenship can emerge. Walzer (1983) has suggested a break with the old normative idealism embodied in collectivist and universal notions of 'the social' and advocated new thinking around pluralist frameworks of complex equality, that involve taking democratic rights beyond traditional conceptions of citizenship.

Behind Walzer's vision is the assumption that culture and society shape the nature of government. This is true to a degree. It is essential to the Tocquevillian vision of the pivotal role of intermediate institutions as a generative force in society. However, an older tradition of thought, stretching from Aristotle to Montesquieu, suggests that fundamentally the state shapes civil society, not the other way round. If we accept this view we are thinking not about civil society in the all-embracing sense envisaged by Tocqueville, but about the Roman virtue of *civitas*; that is, public-spiritedness, sacrifice for the community and of course, active citizenship. As Giddens (1998: pp. 79–80) acknowledges, 'there are no permanent boundaries between government and civil society'. Ultimately, it is the state – in particular, entitled citizenship via the welfare state – that provides the conditions in which both democracy and civic life flourish.

At the core of contemporary debates about civil society is the relationship between welfare and citizenship. Much of this debate has turned around a crude distinction between individualism and collectivism. The moral and emotional meanings attached to both terms have obscured as much as they have enlightened. Inherent in the debate about these social forms lies a deeper distinction concerning alternative conceptions of the self, the good life, and human potential and purpose. As Marquand puts it:

> On the one side of the divide are those who view the self as a static bundle of preferences and the good life as one in which individuals pursue their own preferences without interference from others. On the other are those for whom the self is a governing and developing moral entity and the good life one in which individuals learn to adopt higher preferences in place of lower ones. On one side of the divide stress is laid on satisfaction; on the other on effort, engagement and activity. (*Guardian*, 28 October 1996)

In this prescient comment, Marquand essentially differentiates between the independent citizen and the *active* citizen. The active citizen forms the cornerstone of civil society, since he or she has embraced a form of 'solidary individualism' that addresses the imperative of the common good.

The relative influences of individualism and collectivism have waxed and waned throughout the short history of the post-war welfare state. Over the same time, the links between welfare, individual citizenship and notions of public good have been conceived in different ways. Advocates of the early welfare state enthusiastically embraced the concept of the entitled citizen, whose rights to healthcare, housing, education and a guaranteed income went hand-in-hand with a rigorous Fabian ethic of duty. The redistribution of wealth, on which the welfare state edifice rested, would help to create a just and therefore moral social order. Moreover the entitled citizen must also be an active citizen engaged with the community, since social and economic welfare provided the conditions in which the citizen could live an active, informed and fulfilling life.

By the mid 1970s a moral vacuum had opened between the rhetoric and the reality of the welfare state. Into this vacuum stepped anti-collectivists who denounced the welfare state for creating a dependency culture and sapping the moral fibre of society. Marquand has observed that the welfare state, in the eyes of its critics, had produced a hedonistic society, in which collective action and collective provision had become sources of 'moral escapism', encouraging those who took part in them to shelter from the consequences of their own actions – such critiques had the effect of engendering 'a corrosive culture of guilt' (*Guardian*, 28 October 1996).

But this moralistic individualism, based on perceived Victorian virtues of self-reliance and enterprise, proved to be as fragile and even more ephemeral in its influence. A moral order founded on the market is a contradiction in terms, since the market is by definition amoral, antinomian and subversive of all values – except the value of free exchange. The moral individualism of Thatcherism and Reagonomics quickly mutated into hedonistic individualism. The rhetoric of self-reliance and patriotic sacrifice stood in stark contrast to the selfish vices of wealth accumulation and its accompanying lifestyle of self-gratification at all costs.

## Civic trust and social capital

Not surprisingly, as we entered the 1990s a new debate began about the values of civic trust. In this debate, the good society was recast in terms of *civil society*. Such a development represented a swing back towards a kind of collectivism, specifically in the promotion of new forms of communitarianism (Etzioni, 1993; Fukuyama, 1996). However, to describe this trend as a re-assertion of the collectivist values associated with the welfare state would be simplistic. What the 'new communitarianism' of the exponents of civil society sought was to reconcile the globalized market with a form of active citizenship in which the individual pursues moral commitment through involvement in the community. In a sense, this is a cross-cutting definition that defies the distinction between individualism and collectivism. That is both its strength and its weakness.

The exponents of civil society in the contemporary debate about the moral economy of welfare view reciprocal responsibility and social well-being as the basis of 'social capital'. Fukuyama (1996: p. 26) asserts that:

Social capital is a capability that arises from the prevalence of trust in a society or certain parts of it. It can be embodied in the smallest and most basic social group, the family, as well as the largest of all groups, the nation, and in all other groups in between. Social capital differs from all other forms of human capital in so far as it is usually transmitted through cultural mechanisms like religion, tradition or historical habit.

Social capital, therefore, comprises the institutional relationships of a vibrant civil society, based on solidary individualism and active citizenship, from extended families to neighbourhood networks, community groups to religious organizations, youth clubs to parent–teacher associations, local businesses to local public services, playgroups to the police on the beat (Commission on Social Justice, 1994: pp. 307–8). At the heart of this conception of civil society lie values of empathy, compassion, trust and participation. This is the basis of the 'good society' that we all, it is held, yearn to belong to in the midst of uncertainty, scepticism, disillusionment and institutional fragmentation. In this context, the pluralization of lifestyles and the search for meaning in the midst of uncertainty has stimulated a revitalization of the classical concept of civil society as a means for resolving a range of problems within contemporary society.

The renewal of civil society has been associated with demands for a larger role for voluntary welfare provision in both Western societies and the former Soviet Bloc. The voluntary sector is perceived as: (i) an alternative to state bureaucracy and professional elitism, and (ii) a public space between government and market. Civil society in its reinvigorated form is presented by its advocates as a democratic sphere based on concepts of active citizenship, as opposed to the dependent status imposed by the entitled citizenship of the welfare state (Etzioni, 1993).

Within prevalent conceptions of civil society, communities, neighbourhoods, voluntary associations and churches are the basic building blocks of society because they teach civic virtues such as trust and co-operation (Etzioni, 1993; Fukuyama, 1996; Putnam, 1993a). These 'new communitarians' promote the fostering of intermediate institutions – as well as families, neighbourhoods and schools – in civil society. Such intermediate institutions are viewed as a source of moral and social cohesion in a globalized market society. At the same time, a revitalized civil society might be seen as a bulwark against an overweening welfare state that has lost legitimacy due to its remote bureaucratic structure and domination by professional elites. As Landry and Mulgan (1995: p. 6) put it:

> Associational life in the form of family networks, networks of interest groups and others has often provided an important glue through which the individual and the group have been bound together in some larger whole. Traditionally, this 'civic' realm has provided the means for people to transcend pure individual self interest in the name of the public good. More recently, as the state has lost its legitimacy as the upholder and arbiter of that public interest, other types of civic association have come to seem more important.

## Voluntary organization, civil society and the state

Claims for the value of association are not confined to local networks. Salamon (1994; 1998) suggests that a 'virtual associational revolution' is producing a global voluntary sector. This sector is comprised of diverse institutions that share several core characteristics – they are: (i) structured organizations; (ii) located outside the formal apparatus of the state; (iii) not intended to distribute profits to shareholders or directors; (iv) self-governing; and (iv) involve significant private voluntary effort (Salamon, 1994: p. 5).

The impetus for this 'global associational revolution' has come both from the bottom-up and from the top-down. Eastern Europe provides the most dramatic example, with organizations such as Solidarity in Poland and the Civic Forum Movement in Czechoslovakia capturing the imagination of the world. Less well reported were environmentalist movements in Eastern Europe during the Communist era: the Danube Circle, for instance, which opposed the siting of a hydroelectric plant on the Danube in Hungary, and Arche, the environmental organization that campaigned against acid rain in East Germany by tying thousands of bed sheets to apartment roofs and then recording the pollution accumulated. These activists in Eastern Europe (including the Soviet Union) understood 'their efforts as the creating of a "civil society", a society in which individuals have the right not only to speak out as individuals but also to join together in organizations' (Salamon, 1994: p. 5).

This pressure for bottom-up change through voluntary organization was perhaps most dramatic in Eastern Europe because of its role in undermining communist forms of government and their hegemonic system of control. However, Salamon's 'virtual associational revolution' is by definition a global movement touching most continents. Urban popular movements in Mexico and elsewhere in Latin America are characteristic of grassroots political activities against government oppression in the Americas. In Africa, a new wind of change has given rise to grassroots political and environmental organizations (notably in Nigeria), usually of a non-profit and voluntary nature. Chopko, the Indian environmentalist movement, arose from a spontaneous effort by rural residents to protect an endangered forest literally by linking their arms around it.

Support in the West for the expansion of voluntary organizations is distinctive because of its top-down character and its association with the scaling down of the welfare state. Neo-conservatives were at the forefront of this process, notably Margaret Thatcher in Britain and Ronald Reagan in the United States. Reagan opposed 'big government' *per se*. Thatcher took a more radical line by calling for the dismantling not only of the welfare state, 'but also the organised voluntary sector [so as to] leave social care wholly to volunteers' (quoted in Salamon, 1994: p. 8). She described volunteers as 'the heart of all our social welfare provision' (ibid.). Support for voluntarism has not been unique to neo-conservative governments. The Socialist President of France, François Mitterand, sought to liberalize taxes on 'social economy' organizations during the 1980s. However, social economy organizations in France (like Germany) are 70 per cent supported by public funding, creating a symbiotic relationship between the state and the voluntary or community sectors.

Critics of these political conceptions of civil society point out that the real emphasis is on the dutiful citizen engaged in self-help. In contexts of atomized individualism and a fragmented social order, there is an element of unreality about the larger claims made for the concept of civil society as an alternative to state welfare. As Kramer (1981: p. 283) puts it:

Voluntarism is no substitute for services that can best be delivered by government, particularly if coverage, equity and entitlements are valued, there is a danger that those who have jumped on the bandwagon of the era of limits, signalling the end of the welfare state by advocating more voluntarism, are being co-opted by others who share less concern with social justice than with tax reduction.

Moreover, there is persuasive evidence of decline in civic partici- pation amongst the most marginalized in stark contrast to the more affluent. Giddens (1998: p. 82) observes:

> Significantly, however, most of the increase in civic activity has happened among the more affluent strata. People from poorer backgrounds are more likely to centre their informal social contacts upon close kin. Much smaller proportions of people in the more affluent groups suffer from complete absence of social support than those in the poorer strata ... One of the prime concerns of government involvement should be to help repair the civil order among such groups.

Clearly, it is quite unsustainable to suggest that the needs of the most disadvantaged can be met by the voluntary sector. Civil society based purely on the principle of private altruism would not be a civilized society. Indeed, there is no essential link between civil society and civilized society – contrary to Paine's view. Civil society has had a chequered political history. The Nazi party undermined the Weimar Republic in Germany by infiltrating local organiza- tions. It should not be forgotten that both the Mafia and the Ku Klux Klan are intermediate institutions. Paramilitary organizations in Northern Ireland have exerted considerable influence in their communities by establishing a significant presence within some voluntary organizations. At a more general level, some small local groups in Ireland have been thoroughly illiberal in their responses to drug users or people with HIV. Pseudo-religious cults, with their internal cultures of intimidation, psychological domination of the individual and sometimes violent agenda, further highlight the dark side of associational life. In a climate of increasing ethnic conflict, manifested in Europe by communal hostility towards asylum seekers and political refugees, intermediate institutions can be anything but civil.

It is the core contention of this chapter that a form of civil society that is genuinely *civilized* is meaningless outside a welfare state ethos. To argue that Rotary Clubs, Red Cross chapters and local community groups can provide social protection in an era of globalized capital is an untenable position. As Putnam (1995a; 1995b) suggests, civic participation in the home of Tocquevillian values – the United States – is in decline. However, civil society connected to generative political strategies, based on more complex ideas of equality and a more empowering concept of citizenship, can provide a vibrant and powerful concept of civic renewal in an era of social fragmentation. This is a vision of civil society as integral to a welfare state ethos, in which voluntary action prospers in a mixed economy of welfare; in partnership (rather than competition) with the state and social citizenship. The European Union's Comité des Sages (1996: p. 14), which addressed the future of civic and social rights in Europe, shares this vision, stating that while in a global economy competitiveness is a 'fixed imperative', it 'cannot be improved by dismantling the welfare state'. Instead it placed emphasis on developing social rights and 'rejuvenating social dialogue'.

Pluralism is at the core of this vision. The Report of the Commission on the Future of the Voluntary Sector in the UK (Deakin, 1996: p. 22) observed in this regard that 'the pluralism that is a characteristic of a healthy civil society implies a diversity of ideas, institutions and interests that sometimes appears chaotic'. This 'creative chaos', as Ralf Dahrendorf has put it, goes to the heart of the democratic contribution that the voluntary sector makes to the dynamic of civil society. The British social policy scholar, David Donnisson, told the Commission on the Future of the Voluntary Sector (Deakin, 1996: p. 22) that:

> What could become damaging tyrannies and abuses should be kept in check, partly by strong democratic civic leadership, which establishes and polices the limits of tolerable behaviour and ensures that groups that might be neglected gain a hearing and partly by competition between agencies expressing different interests and views. If this system includes a sufficiently rich and

well informed mixture of agencies capable of working in these ways and power holders in the public and private sectors are capable of responding to them, it will help to make the society in which it operates more democratic.

The Commission (Deakin, 1996: p. 15) itself concluded in this regard that 'the relationship between voluntary bodies and democratic institutions can be seen in different ways – either as a contribution in their own right to the vitality of civil society or as a check on abuses of power'.

The EU Comité des Sages (1996: p. 53) went a great deal further; asserting that 'democratic consultation must give due weight to the traditional social partners but cannot be restricted to them alone. It must also encompass new players, and in particular non-governmental organizations'. What is clear is that the voluntary sector is characterized not only by its separation from market or state, but by an internal diversity that potentially contributes to civil society in different ways and at different scales. Citizens contribute to the voluntary sector both as individuals and collectively, informally and formally through organizations, through the giving of time or of money, without payment or as salaried staff. Voluntary organizations operate at national levels and at local or community levels, in myriad forms both large and small. Some are traditional and paternalistic. Others are transparently democratic, controlled and operated by users. Many voluntary organizations have close partnership relationships with the state, often depending on statutory funding for survival. Yet others challenge the state through vigorous social movements that may be seen as constituting 'a people's opposition' (for example, through varieties of environmental, peace, gay and lesbian, feminist, anti-racist action, and so on). In this diversity lies the strength, but also the weakness of the voluntary sector and, indeed, the limitations of civil society in providing a coherent alternative to the welfare state. The mainstream of the voluntary sector in the social market economy is clearly shaped by its symbiotic relationship with the state.

While the struggles of Eastern European dissidents, most famously the Czech playwright Václav Havel, highlighted the threat posed to state-dominated regimes by the informal institutions of civil society, there is a growing sense of the complexity of these issues in changed political circumstances. Havel, installed as President of the Czech Republic following the Velvet Revolution, argued for an 'anti-political politics'. A more sober analysis has emerged of the tide of change that has swept Eastern Europe since 1989. Hann and Dunne (1996: p. 8) have observed that:

> The recent revolutions in Eastern Europe were the first in human history not to be concerned with establishing some form of rational Utopia. These societies (post-communist) are seen as characterised by unfettered egoism and consumerism. Only individuals exist, and they are allegedly devoid of significant human relationships.

Hann and Dunne conclude that 'civil society' was no longer, by the mid 1990s, the emotive slogan that it became for many East European intellectuals a decade earlier (1996: p. 9). They cite the ironic figure of Václav Havel in support of their case. Havel (1993) has admitted to the existence of 'post-communist nightmare'. The Hungarian-born philanthropist George Soros, who financed the movement towards a civil society in Eastern Europe during the 1980s, has also been critical of post-Communist society (*Guardian*, 18 January 1997).

Similarly, Anderson (1996: p. 99), writing about the 'mythical archetype' of Siberia, challenges the view 'in both popular thought and in social theory for the complete absence of any kind of autonomously managed or meaningful public space' in Soviet society. He asserts:

> Unlike the coffee houses or political parties in Euro-American society, civil society in Siberia was harboured within different 'citizenship regimes', which formed restricted yet significant channels for economic and political practice. This past tense is deliberate: the assault on forms of civic entitlement and participation has never been greater than within the current politics of privatisation. (Anderson, 1996: p. 100)

The equation of civil society with a generic Euro-American State is clearly an ideological position that has more to do with Cold War politics than serious social analysis. There are, manifestly, various definitions of civil society in the history of social and political thought, as outlined above. But the relevant distinction here rests on a lexical conflict of meaning inherent in the term 'civil society': between 'citizen society' and 'bourgeois society'. As Timothy Garton Ash has put it, in relation to social life in post-unification East Germany – 'this is "civil society" emerging but civil society less as the central European dissidents dreamed of it than as Karl Marx analysed it – the self-defence of the bourgeoisie' (*New York Review*, 5 November 1998).

## State, family and civil society: family values and welfare reform

If civil society conventionally has been marked off from the state, on one side, and the family, on the other, relations between these spheres are being re-worked in complex ways. Most notable here are the 'welfare reform' strategies that have been pursued since the 1980s in a number of advanced capitalist democracies. In various national contexts in Western Europe, North America and Australasia, the impetus towards welfare reform has devolved into vigorous debate about family responsibility that brings into question the moral economy of social policy.

Within these debates, an ethos of individual and family responsibility is set in opposition to 'dependence' upon state welfare. A 'new consensus' between parties and governments of the left and right is formed around a belief that something must be done about long-term welfare dependency. The problem for governmental exponents of welfare reform (as the Blair government in the United Kingdom has learned) is that the level of consensus is very shallow. In reality this 'new consensus' seems to be predicated on the flimsy structure of acceptance by the left of a neo-conservative critique of the welfare state – as epitomized by Blair's politics of the 'third way'. Central to the 'new consensus' thinking is the belief that it is a mistake to provide welfare benefits without imposing on recipients reciprocal obligations to endeavour to become self-sufficient through education, work and responsible family behaviour. In essence, the argument assumes that government can set the moral climate – that properly directed, it can promote a philosophy of self-reliance and moral rectitude for all the citizenry.

What is called workfare in the United States, or welfare to work in Britain, is a centrepiece of the 'new consensus'. Governments of both right and left have been united in their demand that welfare recipients should be required to work (or to participate in work training placements) as a condition of receiving their welfare entitlements. A great deal of attention has focused on single parents (usually single mothers), who were the sole beneficiaries of the main US welfare programme, Aid to Families with Dependent Children (AFDC). Moral crusaders have demanded that young mothers be required to complete their schooling and prepare themselves for the labour market; older mothers (with previous work experience) are expected to find work in the rapidly expanding secondary labour markets – notably in the voluntary sector. If other national strategies have lacked some of the punitive elements of workfare, they none the less have adopted the same emphasis on moving single parents into the labour market – as in the Jobs, Education and Training (JET) scheme in Australia, or the New Deal for Lone Parents in Britain; both introduced under Labour governments.

The conservative US social theorist, Charles Murray, has been at the centre of this debate about welfare reform. Murray (1984) argued that a new welfare-dependent underclass was being spawned by women who were having children out of wedlock. Murray held the welfare state responsible for this supposed moral decline. Politicians of the conservative right have seized upon Murray's analysis to traduce the moral basis of the welfare state and attack single parents. In strikingly similar style, Keith Joseph, a former Conservative Secretary for Social Services in the UK, remarked that women from the 'lower orders' were breeding the delinquents and denizens of the borstals of the future (see *Guardian*, 9 July 1993).

Critics of workfare have argued that it represents a political stick with which to beat women, detecting a deep misogynistic underlying purpose. Very early in these debates, Christine Pratt-Marston, Co-Chair of the US National Anti-Hunger Coalition asserted in this regard:

> Workfare is a 'stick' instead of a 'carrot' and sticks tend to produce hostility, anger and passive resistance. The person or agency forced to use the stick and the poor person – usually a woman – who is hit with the stick are both in no-win situations.

With carrots – education, job training, safe affordable day care and affordable health insurance – sticks would not be necessary and the situation becomes win-win. (*NASW News*, November 1984).

Other radical critics of workfare denounce it as 'slavefare'. Lemann has observed that the welfare reform debate in the United States 'is a polite way of asking what we do about the black underclass' (Lemann, 1986: p. 34). The fact that these kinds of welfare reform are substantially directed at the lifestyles of excluded minority groups raises fundamental questions about their ethical basis.

Ethical questions also arise for the voluntary sector, given the participation of voluntary organizations in a number of national workfare or welfare to work programmes. The Canadian Workfare Watch group argues that workfare 'threatens the entire ethic of voluntarism' (Workfare Watch, 1996: p. 1). It explains its reasoning:

Workfare is one of the most divisive issues ever faced by the voluntary sector. There are numerous issues that the voluntary sector has to consider in relation to workfare. We need to recognise that requiring work outside the home in exchange for social assistance represents a fundamental shift in the nature and purpose of social programs. Workfare moves assistance away from eligibility based on need, towards providing assistance only to those who prove their deservedness through work.

Workfare, as a crusade to promote responsible values and behaviour, at the same time would seem to challenge the basis of an ethical civil society. It evokes former tyrannies in slavery and coercive poor relief stratagems. As such, workfare is arguably the very negation of the values that advocates of civil society purport to support.

The US social critic Noam Chomsky – in his 'roll back' theory of welfare policy – argues that the welfare state's conservative critics, both East and West, have shifted from strategies of containment to outright retrenchment, partly in the guise of expanding the sphere of 'civil society'. He observes: 'For a long time the purpose was to resist and contain human rights and democracy and the whole welfare state framework; the social contract that developed over the years. They wanted to contain it and limit it. Now they feel, in the current period, that they can really roll it back. They'd go right back to the satanic mills, murdering poor people, basically the social structure of the early nineteenth century' (1996: p. 17).

## Trust, the family, and the nature of intimacy

However apocalyptic Chomsky's vision, it would appear to resonate with popular feelings of insecurity or uncertainty in contexts of social and economic fragmentation. Furthermore, as welfare reforms focus on the organization and duties of the family, what might otherwise been seen as a 'private' sphere of trust and intimacy is set up as a problem of government. The search for intimacy in contemporary societies is often negatively presented in terms of popular absorption with the private lives of public figures. Frequently, this preoccupation focuses on breaches of trust. These glimpses into the private lives of the elite offer the rest of us the reassurance that intimate relationships exist in a precarious and fragile state, and cannot be bought and sold like a commodity. Recent debates over 'family values' and over questions of trust – whether centring on the British monarchy or on the US president – have played out in the public arena certain anxieties over the nature of intimacy, the institution of the family, and the terms of trust. If late modern societies are characterized as 'risk societies', then these include risks that pervade our most intimate relationships.

Social modernization has been accompanied by the dissolution of those external supports – such as the bonds of kinship, social duty or religious beliefs – that kept people's concepts of intimacy and identity in place. The consequences of this transformation have undermined our trust in the dependability of others, the safety of childhood, and individuals' sense of personal identity – which is why we are going through something like a collective nervous breakdown. So what now? *Le deluge*? It would seem not. In reality we are witnessing what Giddens (1992) has called the 'transformation of intimacy'. With the dissolution of traditional external supports we are being asked to renegotiate our intimate relationships on the basis of trust.

In modern societies, the connection between intimacy and sexuality is fundamental, unleashing sexuality from traditional functions of procreation. This development has led to the emergence of forms of 'life politics' that assume individuals' emancipation from the fixities of tradition and from forms of patriarchal domination. Life politics essentially is the politics of choice best encapsulated in the feminist slogan, 'the personal is political'. For women this means the end of reproduction as fate, as life politics gives citizens ownership over their own bodies (Giddens, 1991). Certain traditionalists, seeking to colonize the language of liberation, have reacted by calling themselves 'Pro-Life'. Their crusade against life politics has been successful in forcing the legal definition of the duties and obligations of bodily ownership. Ironically, the political and legal successes of the exponents of traditional values have invariably further undermined the absolutism demanded by their rigorous moral idealism. The privatization of sexuality has put its regulation beyond political and social control. Intimacy is no longer part of the public domain.

What is now being demanded is a re-moralizing of social life in modern society based upon the core value of trust. But what of 'trust'? What does it mean in an intimate relationship? Quite simply trust is the transcendent quality that holds the relationship together through the trials and tribulations it is likely to encounter. It surpasses love and care in its depth, touching the foundations of our personal identity. Trust ultimately involves the vesting of hopes in persons or abstract systems on the basis of a 'leap of faith'. Breaches of trust consequently have fundamental implications for the continuity of intimate relationships.

Whether marital, parental or pastoral, intimate relationships are being transformed. The traditional external supports of family and kinship structures are being replaced by the internal quality of trust. There is undoubtedly a purity and fragility about intimate relationships, which exist on the basis of trust alone, that elevates them in terms of moral expectations far above their externally supported counterparts in traditional society. This transformation in our concept of intimate relationships is reshaping society at its very core. It is tantamount to a revolution from within our collective consciousness. That is why it is so painful and yet so hopeful.

## Conclusion

This chapter has argued that contemporary societies increasingly are characterized by processes of detraditionalization and individualization. However, postmodern society, despite tendencies towards fragmentation and polarization, retains capacities for engendering empathy and trust between people. These two faces of the social order are characterized on one side by a set of utilitarian values, such as self-help, embraced by neo-conservatives; and on the other side by a commitment to altruism and mutualism, as the core of civic virtue. These different strands are brought together by exponents of civil society – on both left and right – who commonly view reciprocal responsibility and mutualism as the basis of civic virtue. In this context, a reinvigorated civil society is promoted as an appropriate response to a range of contemporary social problems. It has also been argued that at the heart of a revitalized civil society are intermediate institutions such as family networks and voluntary organizations, and concepts of civic renewal bear heavily on these sectors. In particular, the family has become a major focus within debates over attempts to roll back the welfare state and curtail social citizenship rights. This emphasis on family responsibility stands in stark contrast to wider processes of fragmentation and individualization, and to a crisis of trust in the family that pervades postmodern society.

# 6
# Trust, Risk and the Environment

*Phil Macnaghten*[1]

## Introduction

People are frequently encouraged to help save the environment. No longer is this seen as purely the preserve of major corporations and government. Increasingly, we are told, it is largely up to us to change our habits and become responsible environmental citizens. Over recent years, largely in the form of sustainability initiatives promoted by states, business and environmental groups, we have witnessed a plethora of initiatives aimed at encouraging people to participate in environmental matters.

But such initiatives have apparently met with limited success. By and large, people continue to drive their cars, to throw away tonnes of waste, to travel on exotic holidays, to frequent supermarkets, and generally to act in what would appear to be an environmentally irresponsible manner. In response, the institutional rejoinder has been to seek new ways to inform the public, in the form of public information programmes or the development of indicators intended to highlight key environmental trends. Embedded in such an appeal to information has been the following notions: that environmentally benign behaviour is limited by people's ignorance of the facts; that ignorance of these facts can be rectified by the provision of information by states and corporations; that such information will engender environmental concern; and that such concern will translate into overt personal and political action. But are these assumptions correct?

This chapter reviews empirical research on environmental perceptions that challenges such assumptions and which argues that perceptions of environmental 'risks' are inextricably bound up with wider concerns about social and civic life. It pays particular attention to the institutional dimensions of human engagement with nature; in particular, the ways in which environmental risks, concerns, attitudes, values, senses of responsibility and so on are mediated by people's sense of their longer-standing 'trust' relationships with those organizations which have formal responsibility for the environment.

'Trust' has emerged as a central category in attempts to unravel environmental perceptions. Opinion poll data in the United Kingdom have consistently indicated a public sense of self-conscious confusion and disorientation with respect to environmental issues (Worcester, 1994; 1995). In a 1995 survey, 45 per cent of respondents agreed with the statement 'I don't really understand environmental issues' (Worcester, 1995). Nor do such polls reveal any compensating sense of trust that at least government-funded scientists understand what they are researching. Only 38 per cent of the public responded that they had 'a great deal' or even a 'fair amount' of trust in what scientists working for the government say about environmental issues, compared to 48 per cent who expressed some trust in industry scientists. Thus substantially less than half of those surveyed recorded any trust in what scientists working for industry or government had to say, although an impressive 82 per cent expressed trust in what was said by scientists working for environmental organizations (Worcester, 1995: p. 72). Even more starkly, only 7 per cent of people in socioeconomic group AB (professional and managerial people) said they trust industry's scientists 'a great deal', and just 2 per cent government scientists, compared with 37 per cent of ABs who said they trust environmental scientists a 'great deal' on what they have to say on environmental matters.

To look at ways of combating such cognitive disorientation, a number of policy-sponsored surveys now include questions on 'the provision of information'. UK data suggest that over 85 per cent of respondents would like 'much more' or 'slightly more' environmental information to be provided by Government and manufacturers (Department of the Environment, 1994: p. 142). However, such information is only likely to be believed in conditions of trust. When asked in the most recent Eurobarometer survey about who were 'reliable information sources on the state of the environment' only a miserly 2 per cent perceived industry to be trustworthy, 1 per cent political parties, 6 per cent public authorities. These tiny figures contrasted with 28 per cent who perceived the media to be trustworthy, 41 per cent scientists, and 62 per cent environmental protection associations (CEC, 1995: p. 58).

Such data indicate how issues of trust envelope research on environmental perceptions. But little research has attempted to go behind such data so as to explore the rich interconnections between trust, the changing character of environmental risk, information provision, and forms of civic and political engagement. This chapter examines in a more detailed way the sense in which issues of trust permeate public concerns about the environment, by highlighting qualitative research findings based on in-depth focus group discussions. In the first section it analyses the centrality of trust to a 'new' environmental risk agenda and then goes on to highlight how issues of trust are played out in relation to a particular 'live' environmental controversy, that of genetically modified organisms (GMOs). The chapter concludes by setting out the need for more 'inclusive' and deliberative institutions within which to negotiate official and popular assessments of environmental risk, and to promote forms of public engagement with the politics of environment that go beyond simple distinctions between the 'state' and 'civil' spheres.

## Trust and environmental risk

Recent commentators have suggested that we are moving from an easy politics of the environment to a hard one in which there are likely to be far more losers than winners and which require new levels of cooperation between government, major corporations and the citizenry (Burke, 1997). Furthermore such an agenda is characterized by hazards which are recognized as truly global in scale (Jacobs, 1997; McCormick, 1995); are mediated by the dictates and promiscuity of the mass media (Anderson, 1997; Jamison, 1996); are generated by scientific advance and the increasing pace of industrial innovation, yet riddled with scientific unknowns and uncertainties (Wynne, 1994; 1996); and which reflect wider mistrust in expertise and the formal world of politics (Grove-White, 1997; Rose, 1995). More generally, such changes have been discussed in relation to a 'risk society' thesis in which a wide variety of environmental issues, including ozone depletion, species destruction, global warming, acidification of lakes and forests, nuclear radiation and chemical pollution, have become widely recognized as risks which are complex, global, long-term, often incalculable, and largely invisible to our senses (Beck, 1992; 1996; see also Adam, 1995; Franklin, 1998; Jacobs, 1997; Lash *et al.*, 1996; Macnaghten and Urry, 1998).

As risks transcend the boundaries of sensory perception, and as the contours of risk extend to the very distant and the extraordinarily long term, the public becomes dependent on national and increasingly global expert systems for information, knowledge, images and icons that might enable such processes to be 'interpreted'. Questions of scale, immediacy, expertise and information provide a theoretical context in which to examine in more detail how people themselves make sense of and negotiate environmental concerns, and the complex ways in which such concerns are embedded in daily life.

These issues were explored in a series of focus group discussions (full findings are in the research report, Macnaghten *et al.*, 1995b), at the start of which participants were asked to choose one or two environmental issues that particularly concerned them. This generated substantial discussion of a wide range of issues. Within this range, participants chose and explained problems in terms related to their daily lives and in relation to the identities they presented to the group. Four main points recurred frequently in these opening discussions: people were concerned with environmental changes that were perceived to interfere with their daily lives; they were particularly concerned with unseen and unknown risks, and with the potentially long-term effects of these risks upon human health; they called upon other participants to share in feelings of disgust and loss, including a sense of outrage that the authorities were either unable or unwilling to respond to such concerns; and people recognized the ambivalence of their concerns by engaging in practices often at odds with their beliefs.

In these discussions, people discussed their environmental concerns as being serious at local, national, and global levels. But whatever the level of the problem, most people also presented environmental issues in terms of the ways in which they interfered with their own day-to-day lives. As one man from a professional group from the south of England stated:

M    I suppose there's pollution of rivers, er, the taking away of the common land, the green land, which our I think our children are going to need, er, the growth of motorways, the growth of pollution, I mean, er, my wife suffers from asthma, and it's the fastest growing er, one of the fastest growing afflictions for children now. Er, sewage, is another one, I think the loss of farmland, that the small farmers – it's leading us to er, to lose a way of life which is quite important. I can go on. How many will you need. (Laughter)

M    Just leave some for us. (Laughter)

(Professionals – Sussex)

The perception of increasingly proximate environmental 'risks' in daily life permeated all the group discussions, often expressed in terms of how conventional and formerly taken-for-granted social practices were now considered dangerous. For example, there was discussion over how they (as parents) no longer permitted their children to swim in the sea, of how they could no longer catch flukes or eat fish from local beaches, of the new dangers associated with canoeing or even leaving your washing outside, of the risks associated with car fumes and the health of young children, and of more general local beach, river and car pollution – especially over the last decade or so. The simple 'affordances' of place – the activities or possibilities an environment provides, furnishes or offers – were beginning to be shaped and structured by people's perceptions of a deteriorating environment (Gibson, 1979).

However, the narrative structure of the passage above is also revealing. Especially striking is the metaphor of loss (loss of a way of life, taking away of common land, loss of green land). Such metaphors are implicitly temporal in that they refer to the passing away of valued and cherished ways of life, with expectations of future absences. Such loss reflects a sense of threat over one's historical attachment to place, and in particular threats to the collective memories and reconstructions of place that shape one's sense of continuity with the past and with the landscape. When places no longer afford simple pleasures, and when sensory experience no longer reveals age-old meanings (cows as part of healthy nature, beaches as places for bathing and sunbathing, rivers as places for catching and eating fish, outdoors and sea air as places for healthy living), it is perhaps not surprising that people felt a sense of disgust and outrage. This suggests that our senses fail us not simply in relation to faraway and invisible risks such as nuclear radiation, but also in more everyday, local, and familiar contexts of daily life (Adam, 1995).

Such discussions were generally forthright and emotive, as people spoke of how environmental change had personally affected important aspects of their daily lives, and clearly expected the other people in the group to agree with them. Indeed a shared sense of disgust and loss was perhaps the most common way in which people expressed deteriorating environmental conditions. Two members of the professional group articulate such feelings of loss below.

M    Well, my main gripe is the river. You were just told about the pollution of the sea. It ends up in the river, comes back in the river, and comes up the river, gets even as far as Arundel, and I've had £300 vet's fee for my dog, who goes swimming in the river, and is getting infections out of the water. And all the muck of the day that's coming up from the sea, back up the river, lies on the bank, and it's never cleared.... And it just – the pollution that's lying there, it's just absolutely disgusting.... You see the very fishes getting washed up dead, fish, crabs, the lot, are just getting washed up on to the banks, and when the river rises then it comes up above the flood banks over the top and into the fields. And it just lies there and ferments. The smell there in the summer is absolutely disgusting.

F    Well, mine is sort of the wildlife and the flowers too ... The flowers aren't there any more. You've got the cattle which are still grazing, but even they don't seem to have as much as they used to. It's just been taken away.

(Professionals – Sussex)

In this and other groups, a similar narrative of disgust and regret was expressed about the loss of countryside and valued green spaces, particular plants and wildlife, traditional ways of life, and everyday activities such as swimming. This disgust and loss were presented as both highly personal and inevitably shared, needing little further explanation. The language of loss and outrage thus illustrates people's sense of their own passivity and powerlessness (as in the quote, 'It's just been taken away') to combat such trends, trends which are commonly experienced as both inevitable and troubling.

Though the group discussions typically started with the immediate effects of environmental damage in daily practice, people were also concerned with dangers that were distant, unseen, unknown, or delayed. People were markedly well informed about a wide range of environmental problems, both in Britain and abroad. However, such familiarity did not appear to engender a sense of trust or a heightened sense of personal or ontological security (Giddens, 1990). It led people to feel overwhelmed by the sheer scale of environmental problems, and to the inchoate sense that not nearly enough was being done. One young urban professional stated:

F     Er, there just seems to be so much of it. And you – almost daily you read about er, oil spillages, and waste going into the sea. Or rivers. Not just in this country, world wide. It may not happen every day on our doorstep, but it's certainly happening almost daily throughout the world.

*Mod.* Right, so, the sheer scale of all this?

F     And nobody seems to – well, people do do things about it, but nothing, there's not enough er, the rules aren't there to stop people from doing it.

     (Young professionals – Manchester)

The difficulty this woman had in translating her rather amorphous feelings into words reflects a more widespread confusion felt by many people as to just how serious environmental problems actually are. Such uncertainties were compounded by a new array of environmental risks that no longer could be seen or sensed, and this engendered an increased feeling of dependency upon experts who often failed to tell one the facts. This generated a discussion of the more diffuse sense of risk and insecurity in everyday living. Indeed, if visible signs of environmental risk have unknown and potentially dangerous consequences, the risks associated with invisible and intangible causes are even more troubling. Such fears were voiced by a group of mothers in the north-west of England, in connection with a mysterious film of dust that was occasionally deposited upon washing, and the unknown risks associated with canoeing:

F      I've got some canoes ... I must admit, I've heard that if you fall in the water you can be ill afterwards.... It would be nice to know, to be reassured that you could – without being ill.
F      I worry about this film you see on your car sometimes, in the morning, from the ICI.... We're very close to the ICI, I don't know. This is why it's very worrying. Some mornings you go out and it's like there's a thick layer of dust all over everything.... If it was just a bonfire and they were burning rubbish, and it was just – soot, well you'd think, ah, well it's just – but you don't know what it is. It could be anything couldn't it?
F      Because you can smell something it doesn't mean it's harmful. I mean, probably the ones that are really harmful are the ones you can't smell.
       (Mothers – Lancashire)

Such anxieties about the unknown risks again raise the issue that our senses can no longer be trusted to interpret the dwelt-in world. Such anxieties illustrate the salience of the so-called 'risk society' and a fundamental sense of insecurity. These anxieties were also linked to worries about future effects, especially in relation to what life would be like for one's children.

F      Because we have young children, we just – you just don't know what their life is going to be like. When they are our age, what is going to happen?
       (Mothers – Sussex)

Such passages reveal an apparently shared and widespread loss of faith in the future (see also Macnaghten *et al.*, 1995a). Many of the participants spoke of a future in which there would be fewer jobs, more crime, more cars and pollution, and less countryside. More generally, such sentiments appeared to be connected to a largely sceptical view of the self-interested character of those organizations charged with caring for the environment, and to massive doubts about their ability to act responsibly in awesomely long 'glacial' time. There appeared to be a mismatch between the short-term intentions of those who have power and influence – largely viewed as a perfectly justifiable response to the necessities of modern economic life – and the longer-term dictates of the environment.

However, the people involved in the focus groups had not significantly restructured their lifestyles, nor were they engaged in collective forms of protest or lobbying. The ambivalence of people's responses to environmental threats was time and time again illustrated by their comments about cars. These were identified both as the most visible threat to the environment, and as an essential part of people's daily lives which could not be done without. Most people expressed concerns about car emissions, and how this was affecting their health, referring frequently to the heightened prevalence of asthma in children.

M     With me it's the air pollution. Er, I drive something like 35,000 miles a year, in my job, increasingly I'm conscious of sitting in traffic jams, the North West is probably one of the worst examples in Britain, and has been for the last couple of years.... I am now very, very conscious of breathing in crap all the time. Also, believe it or not, I jog four or five times a week, where I live is half a mile from the M6, a couple of miles from the M61, I'm surrounded by it, and usually I'm jogging maybe about six half past six at night, alongside the traffic, and I can almost taste this stuff.... it's more and more cars, cars, cars.
     (Working man – Lancashire)

This participant and others could express apparently contradictory views on such issues, and expect that the rest of the group would accept this ambivalence. Such ambivalence – using a car while criticising the effects of traffic – is linked to a subjective model of personal agency; that is of how one conceives of one's sense of power to effect change either directly or through trusted institutions. These models of agency are the framework within which people determine the likely efficacy of future action.

Most people accepted that everyone is partly responsible for environmental problems, that solutions might mean far-reaching changes to our personal lifestyles, and that technological and consumer-driven society was not sustainable. However, calls for people to change their individual lifestyles were only occasionally promoted by participants in the focus groups. On such occasions, people tended to stress the need for environmental education, especially of children. The older and rural groups tended to advocate education, with a particular emphasis on teaching young people to care about local and aesthetic environmental issues, such as not throwing litter or letting their dogs mess the pavements.

M    It is discipline at home. You turn that light switch off, you don't need that now – go to the fridge and open a bottle of something and drink half and throw the other half down the sink. Or open a can and some take two sips out and say I don't like it, I don't want it. That's waste. And it's total waste of the material it was made with and the waste of the energy as well.
(Professionals – Sussex)

Other people also spoke of their own personal power to effect change, usually through consumer choices, such as buying dolphin-friendly tuna or aerosols which do not contain CFCs. For some, voting and democratic accountability were still the best means towards a better environment, even though conventional political structures were seen as limited in their capacity to solve environmental problems:

M    We can nibble round the edge of the total environmental issue, but at the end of the day, if we don't get the politics right, if we don't get the power, to be able to control our own environment, then we go nowhere. People don't realise the power of their vote. You are absolutely correct. They [referring to politicians] think of today and tomorrow. They don't think of next week, never mind 350 frigging years. That's how short sighted they are. Now we are going to have to get a grip of it, bloody soon. I think there's a very small, there is a slow awakening as to the environmental issues there, there's a slow awakening, but there is an awakening, I'm a wee bit more encouraged.
(Working man – Lancashire)

But this model of agency was largely absent in the focus group discussions. Rarely did people believe that collective action (through participation in political parties, consumer or environmental groups, or trade unions) would help promote a better environment. More common was the belief that voting rarely changed anything, that real power was largely beyond their control, and that the deteriorating state of the environment was a largely intractable by-product of a system increasingly dictated by financial interests. Such beliefs reflect the widespread distrust of public institutions encountered in the study reported above. For instance, the man who made the ambivalent comment on the usefulness and threat of cars, quoted earlier, continued:

*M*     It's more and more cars, cars, cars. That's from government policy all the way through. And anybody who uses vehicles and has used them for maybe ten or fifteen years must see the massive increase of everything on the road. It's the pollution of the air. And as linked to the previous one [heavy metals] obviously, it's the oil companies again, it's the financial clout of the oil companies.

(Working man – Lancashire)

In the same group, there was much discussion concerning whether states still possessed the authority to manage environmental risks in the face of the power of multinational corporations. The subsequent passage shows just how deep global economic integration has penetrated local consciousness.

*M*     But that's the key to the whole thing, the attitude of the whole thing. It's all politics, it's economics, and it's power. And the power of the multinationals who are involved in oil, who are involved in gas exploration, they make and break governments, it's as simple as that. And if in fact the government is not going to really make it difficult for a company who employ nearly 50 thousand people and donate several million to the war chest the next general election, then what chance have you got of real legislation – who will punish someone who's dumping tens of thousands of barrels of crap into the sea? They won't do it.

(Working Men – Lancashire)

This model of increasingly global and hegemonic capitalist interests informed much of the discussion of the environment, including the likelihood of solutions and what people themselves could or should do. For example, many people spoke of how it was unfair to blame individuals when big companies were themselves mostly to blame, of how there was insufficient regulation of industry by governments, and of how environmental degradation in the developing world was possibly even more serious where companies could get away with it more easily. This cynical view of industry and governments was commonplace in all the discussions, frequently in a similar form to the assertion made in the Lancashire mother's group, 'at the end of the day, it's all down to money, isn't it?'

This study examined how people make sense of environmental issues and the factors that mediate the complex relationship between concern and action. Contrary to much survey research which has suggested a decline in the public salience of 'the environment' we found that people from many sectors of society were aware of a wide range of issues, and were deeply concerned about them. Moreover, these anxieties were exacerbated by a sense of environmental risks becoming increasingly uncertain, unknowable, globalized, and dependent upon highly abstract expert systems. Furthermore, there was a common perception that these risks were beginning to impact directly upon people's health and to constrain locally based social practices. We now move to a more specific study which addressed the factors underpinning people's concerns regarding genetically modified organisms.

## Trust and biotechnology

In this section key findings are set out from a qualitative research study on public perceptions of biotechnology (full findings are in the research report, Grove-White *et al.*, 1997). Here, the focus lies on the ways in which trust has become a central factor within such debates, mediating the tangled and changing relationships between science, the environment and government.

Public unease with biotechnology since the late 1990s, and with GM foods in particular, reflects a symbolic landmark in the risk society debate. It reflects *par excellence* a risk, invisible to our senses, whose future trajectory is highly complex, largely unknown, perhaps incalculable, and where the long-term impacts on the environment and human health may be serious, perhaps even irreversible in potentially altering the life-conditions of future generations in ways which respect neither national boundaries nor class divisions. Furthermore, the application of gene technology into the sinews of everyday life is symbolic of the mounting reliance that we all face on the judgements of 'experts' in conditions of perpetual technological innovation and technological change. Trust in public institutions, in the regulatory apparatus, in the science underpinning the development, in the corporations promoting the technology, in the food manufactures and retailers selling the GM foods, becomes a sine qua non for public acceptability.

At the start of the first set of focus group discussions we introduced the concept of biotechnology and explored people's responses, in relation to the concept in general, and in its application to various product lines. The dominant reaction in all groups was negative. A range of responses arose: that genetic modification constituted 'meddling' with nature and should be avoided; that BSE illustrated the unforeseen hazards which could arise from such meddling; that such interference with nature illustrated the extent to which industry, science and technology had permeated daily life; that the supposed benefits were for the commercial interests promoting the technology rather than the consumer; and that such developments caused them to feel wary, suspicious and to wonder 'why'?

F    It sounds dangerous and unnatural.... I get the impression that all the food's been meddled with in a laboratory before it reaches the supermarket. It doesn't interest me at all. It's like all these, you know these fruits that they inject with stuff to keep the apples redder for longer and things. I want food to be fresh, I don't want it to have all this stuff in it.... But that's like scientifically taking natural food and making it unnatural.
(North London Working Mothers)

F    It's like an interference with nature. Although they may say that it will be better, how do you know it is going to be better, because you don't know what they've done to it, do you? So I'd be very untrusting of it really.... I mean anything to do with genetics is frightening, isn't it, really? [In what way is it frightening to you?] Well because they cannot prove that if it's new, then they haven't had time to do any tests, have they, over a number of years.
(Lancashire Non-Working Mothers)

Such responses indicate considerable unease and general mistrust of the technology as a whole. For some, the modification of genes was simply wrong and immoral, representing a form of 'meddling' which transgressed people's implicit sense of the order of things. Such people tended to highlight the inherent foolishness of such attempts at playing God. However, most people's responses were more discriminating, especially in relation to particular products. For example, despite their generally acknowledged unfamiliarity with the technology, most participants were at pains to distinguish between classes of product and the different issues, positive and negative, these raised for them. Significantly, the character of response for a particular type of product often related to the purpose to which that product would be put. Medical products tended to be seen as relatively acceptable because of the health benefits they would bring, overriding unease about other features felt to be of concern when applied to less socially disinterested uses. Similarly, the general argument that biotechnology could help alleviate food shortages in developing countries appeared to carry strong moral weight (tempered by occasional scepticism), overriding other more 'local' concerns. By contrast, forceful moral repugnance was expressed towards particular gene transfers across species – from animals to plants and, more emphatically still, between humans and either animals or plants. In general, the anxieties were more pronounced, the closer particular proposals came to challenging people's sense of an established moral order.

People's more general sense of trust or mistrust of the technology as a whole reflected their sense of the social conditions in which it was apparently being introduced. For many participants, the BSE crisis was mentioned in support of people's expressions of unease at various dimensions of biotechnology. The risks of GM foods tended to be seen as of the same class of risk as BSE – in terms of unnaturalness, the failure of institutions to prevent them, the long-term character of associated risks, and our inability to avoid them. The analogy with BSE was especially drawn upon to illustrate how 'unnatural' interventions may have unforeseen and dangerous long-term consequences, as when cattle were fed sheep and other mammalian offal. Turning cows into carnivores (and at times cannibals) was seen as dangerous meddling, and the long shadow of BSE had demonstrated the power of nature to 'strike back'. Genetic modification sounded like a similar scale of interference with natural processes, leading many people to expect harmful effects in the long-term:

F   Well they seem to come up, you hear more and more things, I think you do personally, but everybody's denying what caused BSE and that it's something to do with unnatural processes with animal foods as far as I understand it.
F   Forcing natural herbivores to eat meat.
F   Yes and I just think it's unnatural. Is it good for you?
F   I think we're worried basically about the safety aspects.
    (North London Working Mothers)

The BSE crisis was also mentioned in relation to people's mistrust of official reassurances of safety. Not only was the recent history of official handling of that crisis used to illustrate a perceived tendency towards mendacity and 'cover-up' where powerful industrial interests were at stake, but it was also held to show the unreliability of 'scientific' reassurance in such fields. Certain individuals were explicit about the educative role the crisis had served in dispelling their 'innocence' about such matters.

*M*   If anybody said to me before that they were feeding cattle with cattle, I never knew anything about that, that information wasn't available to me. I would have said without a doubt that that isn't right.

*Mod.* Has BSE affected how you think about food?

*M*   I think so.

*M*   It's probably affected our trust in the people who are presenting food stuff to us, more than the food itself I would have thought. You know, less likely to trust a politician that's force feeding a youngster on a hamburger just to try and prove that it's perfectly, you know, that the food's safe to eat. So it sort of sows the seed of doubt in their capabilities of telling us the truth.

   (Lancashire Risk Takers)

There is perhaps an additional way in which people's experiences of the BSE crisis has contributed towards a general sense of mistrust, concerning the mismatch between the character of public anxieties over what is implicated and the more restrictive criteria used in official risk pronouncements. Whereas government and industry have tended to defer responsibilities for policy development to scientific assessments of risk, as if science is equipped to provide unmediated and normatively compelling judgement, people's concerns have tended to be wider in scope and remit. In the case of BSE these included: the morality of feeding the by-products of dead animals back to natural herbivores, general issues of the industrial intensification of foods, the proximity of parts of government to producer interests, and so on. Similarly in the GM sphere, whereas government and industry tend to suggest that the technology can and should be managed safely on a 'case-by-case' basis, people have harboured significant concerns about the technology as a whole, relating to its justification, need, benefit and context of use; as well as more general unease over the trustworthiness of regulatory provisions and institutions themselves. In both cases, such wider social and moral concerns have tended to be excluded from public debate largely due to Britain's reductionist culture of risk assessment (Wynne, 1996).

It should be stressed, however, that the BSE experience cannot be seen as the cause of public anxieties about GMOs in the food context. Rather it seemed to serve as a condensed symbol, or heuristic, around which previously more diffuse and abstract concerns could be articulated. Thus, it served variously at different points in the discussions as a focal point for referring to the unresponsiveness of the official regulatory system, for suspicions about the 'capture' of that system by private interests, for the misleading character of scientific statements about 'no evidence of harm', and for the 'unnaturalness' of tendencies in modern food production. On the evidence of these discussions, there seems little doubt that the episode has been something of a watershed in public consciousness in the United Kingdom – as much for the way in which it encapsulated concerns about recent syndromes and trends of which people had previously been aware in less focused fashion, as because of any precise historical sequence of events that occurred.

In relation to the technology as a whole, people felt a considerable sense of fatalism and powerlessness. The development of genetically modified foods appeared to be seen as lying outside their own boundaries of control, with little space for public choice or intervention. These feelings of inevitability seemed to reflect a felt absence of choice and a sense that, realistically speaking, driven as it was by powerful financial interests, the technology was unstoppable. Such 'inevitability' appeared to lie behind feelings of passive resignation in the majority of the groups:

F    Well that one because it makes me feel I'm not actually in control of this. I have no control over this. It's gonna happen and I can't ... You know.
      (Lancashire Non-Working Mothers)
F    It makes me feel really that we don't have a lot of choice, that things will move this way and eventually we will have to accept it.
      (Lancashire Church Goers)

Since government and industry were perceived not be trusted to develop biotechnology in a fashion sensitive to their concerns, what emerged from the focus groups was that the role of public guardian in practice was played by non-governmental organizations – and, in particular, by Greenpeace (which was mentioned spontaneously in several of the groups):

*F* Because they're looking at the overall picture – the whole environmental issue and everything. Not just making money, making things grow bigger, faster and everything else.
*Mod.* So Greenpeace would be quite important because it's not governed by money?
*F* They're our voice, aren't they? They're another way ... They educate us even more. I mean, the politicians tell us things that we know ... We know they're lying,. They're out to line their pockets or fit their own ends.
*F* Greenpeace are political as well.
*F* Yes, but how political are they? They're not political for the people; they're political for the planet. Basically, I'm not ... I'm not a big environmentalist or in Greenpeace, but that's only because I'm too lazy to get off my arse and do something about it. I'm bloody glad there are people out there doing it ...
*F* Oh. Yeah, yeah.
*F* Damned glad ...
   (Lancashire Non-Working Mothers)

All of this suggests that at the core of much of the unease about biotechnology uncovered in the groups are important questions of trust. Throughout the discussions there were copious indications of mistrust of official institutions, of official claims of safety, of the regulatory framework, of the intentions of those promoting the technology, and of the supposed benefits claimed by protagonists. Indeed, such findings are becoming a commonplace of social research and opinion polls in contemporary Britain. Significant though these findings are however, they need to be strongly qualified, particularly in the context of discussion about the commercial diffusion of genetically modified organisms.

The fact is, quite as striking as the mistrust and even cynicism expressed towards official bodies and spokesmen, was an apparent expectation that government could and should be capable of acting authentically in the public interest on such matters, notwithstanding recent perceptions of contrary tendencies. In other words, there appears to be considerable ambivalence about the expectations people have of government in relation to 'risk' issues like those raised by biotechnology as applied to food.

At one level, it may be reasonable to see this ambivalence as a reflection of the extent to which people feel trapped by their own dependency upon such official 'expert' systems, and are realistic about this fact. Thus increasingly in domains of this kind, people may now be exhibiting a form of 'virtual' trust in relation to regulators, acting *faute de mieux* 'as if' they feel trust, because of a realistic sense of lack of alternatives in circumstances of all-embracing and non-transparent dependency on expert judgements (Grove-White *et al.*, 1997). If this is correct, a likely corollary is the potential brittleness of the 'as-if' trust generated thereby, since the latter is not rooted in authentically deep-rooted confidence based on positive experience, nor in any expectation of agency in relation to ensuring the proper behaviour of official regulators. Given this brittleness, an obvious concern arises – that, in the event of things going wrong in the GMO sphere, conventional patterns of official reassurance will lack purchase; leading in turn to a loss of control and other perverse feedbacks for politicians and the political system more generally.

However, the same public ambivalence may also have a less discouraging side. For it suggests the persistence of a strong residual public belief that our political institutions are capable, at least in principle, of responding to new circumstances and needs. Nevertheless, the challenges in the GMO domain in this regard appear very substantial. In several of the groups there were strong indications that people felt their own lurking concerns – for example in relation to the moral implications of the species 'boundary' being transgressed, and the issue of 'irreversibility' should present scientific assurances about GMOs in food prove faulty – were not being acknowledged by those responsible. This manifested itself in occasional despair and despondency:

F    I started out not too bad when I had the discussion. I thought I'd have an open mind about it, but I've changed my mind. As soon as I saw that about the human gene, suddenly the enormity of it made me feel really awful. I got an awful feeling about it, because I thought it was something that … I think we're touching things that we don't realise and I think that we're taking things out of the earth, and we're now trying to correct it by using things like genetic engineering, because mistakes were made. And I feel that time's just ticking by and we don't realise what's going to happen in the future. I think something terrible could happen. It's given me a bad feeling really.

*Mod.* So it's as if we're trying to fix something which is mixed up with something …?

*F*     Yes, because the earth hasn't got what it used to have. We feel we have to put something back into the food to make it better, and maybe we're correcting things in the wrong way. I don't know …

*F*     It's a frightening thought to think that time's ticking away though …

*F*     Yes. It's something that I'd like to put at the back of my mind now. I wouldn't like to think about it again. I probably wouldn't – but when we talk about it, it does bring it to your mind. But then I'll probably put it to the back of my mind now …

(Lancashire Working Women)

This sequence – while at a literal level apparently interpreting the role of genetic modification in an idiosyncratic way – reflects in heightened, even poetic, form the sense of open-ended uncertainty evoked by discussion of the technology in several of the groups, and the strong feelings of impotence and fatalism this seemed to engender. In such circumstances, unambiguous unilateral assertions by industry and government spokesmen that the technology can and should be managed safely on a 'case-by-case' basis in terms of risk may have the effect of compounding, rather than assuaging, the mistrust felt by individuals across all population groups. Again, there is a body of sociological understanding of such human dynamics, highlighting the ways in which such over-confident official 'body language' can be inflammatory and actively corrosive of public respect for government – for example historically in the sphere of nuclear safety (MacGill, 1987; McSorley, 1990).

The range and texture of the latent concerns hinted at in the group discussions appears to imply a serious continuing challenge for the political process, and more particularly for the established GMO regulatory framework – to demonstrate that the true nature of such concerns (rather than some administratively-contrived reductionist version of them) is being understood, respected and addressed to the maximum extent possible. The alternative, it seems, is a continuing corrosion of trust.

## Conclusion

Beck (1992) claims that in the new 'risk society', risks could no longer be directly touched, tasted, heard, smelt, and especially seen. In this chapter we examined qualitative research data which suggests that for many people this was indeed the case; moreover such risks were now permeating everyday life and contributing to a diffuse sense of unease and insecurity. In these circumstances, 'trust' becomes a crucial mediating factor. In the research studies highlighted, we found that mistrust is even more widespread than previously thought and related to a widespread disaffection with the institutions of science, the media, business, and most significantly the state. Particularly important is the belief that visible signs of environmental risk have unknown consequences, that the senses can no longer be trusted to make sense of daily practice, that all of this belies the true extent of risk on an evolutionary or glacial scale, and that this leads to a fundamental sense of anxiety and pessimism over the future. Such fears are further exacerbated by the strong sense that institutions of the state and business are both unwilling and unable to respond to such concerns.

Such patterns of risk are strikingly in evidence in relation to recent controversies over genetically modified foods in Britain and elsewhere, where important public concerns – largely unacknowledged in the regulatory processes – are arising from acknowledged uncertainties and unknown potential risks from the technologies. Indeed, GMO regulation provides something of a test bed for the capacity of official bodies to respond to significant new public concerns under wider conditions of globalization, free trade and deregulation.

Developing trust, and a sense of common purpose, has become a pivotal question in contemporary politics. So far, there has been minimal attempt in the UK to engage active public involvement in discussion of GM food-related matters with the result, inter alia, that both government and industry in the UK appear to be operating on the basis of seriously limited 'social intelligence' relevant to possible future developments. There appears to be major scope for new institutional experiment in Britain, to stimulate wider discussion and insight about possible positive and negative social and environmental implications of biotechnology as a whole, about the most acceptable product classes of GM food developments, about 'transspecies boundary questions', and about possible 'mishap' scenarios and how these might be mitigated.

More generally, questions of how to rebuild trust in the environmental domain need to be incorporated into the political mainstream. The details of what may be required lie beyond the scope of this chapter. However, from the research highlighted above we may conclude with some preliminary observations. Firstly, the research found a yawning gap between the government's restrictive definition of risk regulation and assessment in the GMO domain, and the far broader character of public concerns. This points to the crucial significance of the need to frame environmental policy in tune with people's own sensibilities and sense of 'what is at stake'. Secondly, such framing relies on developing more attuned forms of 'social intelligence' in a period of substantial change. Tuning into public sensibilities may involve the development of deliberative methods and experiment, including more innovative use of focus groups, citizens panels, citizens juries, consensus conferences and so forth. Such democratic experiments are already under way in attempts to establish more direct forms of contact between citizens and government (see Blair, 1998; Giddens, 1998). The task is to develop and innovate new forms of democratic engagement in the environmental domain.

## Note

1. This paper reports on a body of research conducted over a three to four year period at the Centre for the Study of Environmental Change. The author is indebted to a number of colleagues who collaborated and shared in this research, and to Unilever and the ESRC, who funded the endeavour. A particular debt is owed to Robin Grove-White, Greg Myers, John Urry and Brian Wynne.

# 7

# Trust, Charity and Civil Society

*Peter Halfpenny*

## Introduction

This chapter approaches the concept of trust, its relation to charity, and the place of these in civil society, by a roundabout route. The discussion is partly historical and partly philosophical, based on a belief that in order to better understand the key concepts we should step back from some of the more dominant arguments which currently surround these issues. These include policy debates about the proper functioning of the mixed economy of welfare, with their disputes over the relative responsibilities of the state, private, voluntary (or non-profit) and informal sectors in delivering welfare (Deakin, 1996). Similarly we should step back from current academic debates about trust as the basis of the voluntary associations that, it is argued, are central to the renewal of civil society. Such a renewal is favoured by both left and right, as the embodiment of the moral values which will discipline economic and political institutions by reining in their excesses (see Cohen and Arato, 1992). While trust relations and charitable impulses are today generally seen as socially and politically desirable in themselves, the discussion in this chapter examines how such norms are shaped by particular historical conditions, and fit into larger models of social order.

The chapter begins with a brief synopsis of theories of modern social integration. It draws on a Western perspective developed since the Enlightenment radically transformed people's conception of their world, freeing them from the constraints of traditionalist thought and encouraging them to analyse the bases of social order (Hawthorne, 1976). The purpose of this brief history of ideas is to set out the context within which were fashioned abstract models of economic, political and social order. These models' common dependence on utilitarianism – modernity's central though permanently contested hallmark – leads into some philosophical reflections about the role that trust plays in each of them.

Two conceptions of trust are identified: one (important within utilitarianism) is a subjective probability that renders outcomes of individual actions calculable in conditions of uncertainty; the other (outside utilitarianism) is an essential precondition of social existence, necessary even for utilitarian analyses to succeed. These two conceptions of trust rest on different assumptions about modern social relations – assuming in the first case a model of rational interaction, and in the second a more 'embedded' notion of social integration. Such assumptions produce radically different understandings of how and why people enter into relations of 'trust'.

The discussion takes up a similar historical framework to trace some variations in the notion of charity. Rather than representing a universal norm, concepts of charity are contingent upon particular ways of addressing issues of social obligation, justice and need. Finally, the concluding section reflects philosophically on the implications of the preceding discussion for notions of trust, charity and civil society. It examines the centrality of one conception of trust to the very existence of human society, and the importance of the other conception of trust to utilitarian models of the economy, the polity and the social. It stresses charity's variable expression according to social and historical context. And it notes that the idea of civil society captures the core dilemma apparent in the utilitarian tradition – how best to combine individual freedom with collective benefit. It is not clear, however, that any of these three core concepts provides an adequate solution.

## Civil society and the problem of social integration

Theories of social integration tend to be influenced by the problems and possibilities of the age. Looking back on the awesome transformations in Western societies over the past five hundred years, there is an inspiring abundance of attempts to understand why changes occurred and to articulate programmes for the future. Selecting from this intellectual ferment, the following historical sketch starts by quickly noting a widely held view of premodern society before shoe-horning some of the main theories of social integration developed over subsequent centuries into three broad frameworks which gave prominence, in sequence, to: the economy as the powerhouse of change; the polity as the regulator of the economy; and the social as the bulwark against the perceived excesses of both economy and polity.

In the medieval period up to the sixteenth century, it is widely maintained by social theorists, devotion to a sense of honour sustained the social bonds upon which rested European civilizations. Social harmony was dependent upon the correct performance of the duties and obligations characteristic of one's social category, one's station in life, such as noble, clergy or villein. Each social category or estate had its own code of honour inscribed in its customs and habits, its rituals and routines; its own forms of social inter-dependencies involving courtesies and reciprocities articulated through exchanges of gifts and favours, offices and honours. It was one's proper engagement in these networks of interdependency that vindicated one's claim to honour and demonstrated one's virtue. People were thought of as essentially virtuous, social beings who naturally strove to be honourable in their everyday affairs.

This view was transformed over the seventeenth and eighteenth centuries with the apparently ineluctable rise of what was at the time called 'civil' or 'commercial' society, and the beginnings of what is now called 'modernity' (see Becker, 1994). Religious dissent and growing scepticism eroded confidence in the constraining certainties of the past. People were no longer conceived as naturally inclined to sociability but instead as self-directed. Cohesive moral communities fractured and were replaced by individualized free-thinkers who formed their own social networks and voluntary associations according to their tastes and interests. Community-based codes of honour faded to be replaced by individual conscience. Honour was diluted to no more than individual honesty. Wants were no longer regulated by community mores but were under the sole authority of the individual. Rational calculation displaced customary practice in determining one's engagement with the natural and social world. Improvements in agriculture, transport and manufacturing, alongside the extension of the money economy and a free market, brought increasing prosperity, at least to some.

Commentators were ambivalent about the changes they observed as agricultural communities transmuted into industrial nations (see Hawthorne, 1976). Economic advances were accompanied by the extension of private property with its owners' right to exclude access to it by others, which increased inequalities. Alongside this, the specialization of labour weakened conviviality and social solidarity. Community and common property were being replaced by 'a society of strangers' enjoying their private pleasures. There was much discussion of how best to balance benevolence and self-interest, collective welfare and individual rights (see Seligman, 1992). Some thought that paternalistic government was necessary to regulate individual wants through interventions in the market in order to create security and prevent instability. Others thought that the impersonal hidden hand that equilibrated markets would create harmonious public order out of individuals' untrammelled pursuit of their self-interest and accordingly that no supra-individual institutions were required (see Polanyi, 1957).

By the middle of the nineteenth century, evaluations of civil society – in its older sense of the commercial economy – were less favourable, as its costs were increasingly seen to threaten its benefits. Crowded cities, pauperization, epidemics and widespread wretchedness forced themselves upon social commentators' attention (see Kent, 1981). Commercial self-interest had been carried by the force of competition to the point of inhumanity. The burgeoning economy was having a corrosive effect on society. This prompted a wide range of responses, from the revolutionary to reformist to conservative, as theorists struggled to identify how nations might reap the benefits of plenty without the accompanying degradation of individuals and desiccation of community life. Whatever visions social theory projected, in practice the struggle was between those who wanted to strengthen the state, giving it powers to regulate and control the abuses wreaked by free markets, and those who believed that all political interventions prevented equilibration of the economy and introduced the distortions responsible for suffering and want. The position adopted influenced political design. The *laissez-faire* view underpinned models of liberal democracy, with their etiolated political administrations, representative (through periodic elections) of the people's will, and charged principally with securing the rights of their citizens. The interventionist doctrine, on the other hand, favoured statist models wherein powerful central bureaucracies took responsibility for managing the economy in the collective interests of the citizens.

In the late twentieth century, with each of these political forms in 'crisis', a renewed conception of civil society was widely canvassed as offering solutions (Cohen and Arato, 1992). The crisis of Communist regimes in Eastern European countries was taken by many to demonstrate the power of voluntary associational formations and social movements to overcome the excesses of totalitarian states without adopting a neo-liberal or libertarian stance that the economy should be given free reign (see Blackburn, 1991; cf. Keane, 1988b). In parallel, it was proposed that the liberal democracies of the West – still host to a substantial, socially excluded and impoverished underclass despite vast spending on welfare provision – could also benefit from strengthening the social realm to provide a bulwark against the destructive forces of a capitalist market economy which both exacerbated inequalities and wreaked widespread environmental damage.

Political administrations in liberal democracies were failing to supply this bulwark; indeed they either implicitly colluded with the economy against the people through cross-membership and shared interests, or imposed their own increasingly rigid mass 'solutions' that did not satisfactorily attend to the diversity of their constituencies. This latter charge, for example, was levelled against the municipal socialism of local government in the United Kingdom, with its unsuccessful social housing estates and failing schools. According to the advocates of this new notion of civil society, no longer was it a matter of championing the economy over the polity or vice versa; instead there was a 'third way', the promotion of civil society through which people can wield influence over both (Giddens, 1998). Civil society in this renewed sense comprises social intercourse, free communication and association; independent of, yet influential upon, economic organizations of production and consumption on the one hand, and political parties and state administrations on the other.

## Three models of social action

The simplified brief history set out above is drawn in broad strokes and it is undoubtedly tendentious. Nevertheless, the three phases of modernity identified as unfolding over the past three or four centuries, where prominence was given first to the economy, then to the polity, and finally to the social (or civil society), provide the materials out of which modernist thinkers, committed since the Enlightenment to progressive human improvement through rational calculation, have constructed abstract models of three facets of human action.

First, the economy (or civil society in its seventeenth century meaning), where the neoclassical micro-economic model has today become the orthodoxy. This model is based on three core utilitarian assumptions about how individuals, and more generally other agents such as households and firms, make decisions and interact (Smart and Williams, 1971). The first assumption is that individuals have a relatively stable set of underlying preferences and their well-being (or utility) improves the more these preferences are fulfilled. The second assumption is that individuals act entirely selfishly in seeking to maximize their own well-being subject only to limits imposed by their available resources. In other words, within the constraint of their budget, individuals act rationally on the basis of full information to maximize their benefits and minimize their costs, regardless of the welfare of others.

The third assumption is that market trading co-ordinates the actions of different individuals; unfettered markets tend towards a general economic equilibrium in which all supplies of and demands for goods and services are ultimately perfectly co-ordinated. The result is optimally efficient because it achieves the greatest collective satisfaction of preferences, in that no-one can be better off without someone else being simultaneously worse off. The benefit of the elegant simplicity of this model is that it makes tractable a wide range of people's activities; it is possible to calculate the outcomes – what people will do – given knowledge of their preferences and their participation in the market.

An analogue of the neoclassical micro-economics model is implicit in one model of the polity: representative democracy (or democratic elitism). This theory is founded on the view that legitimate government derives from the voluntary consent of all the free individuals who make up the governed, and not from the divine, heritable or traditional rights enjoyed by only one or some of the people, such as the monarch or the aristocracy. Nevertheless, it recognizes that the classical ideal of participatory democracy, involving communal self-government by the whole citizen body – through for example popular assemblies – cannot operate in modern nations because of their complexity and size. Instead, political elites or parties enter their manifestos into the market place, and members of the electorate periodically 'buy' through their votes the one that closest fits their individual preferences. The return for the successful party is power – the right to govern – just as profit is the return in the economy. This model of representative democracy incorporates three utilitarian principles parallel to those of neo-classical micro-economics (Downs, 1957; cf. Green and Shapiro, 1994). First, people have policy preferences and their welfare improves the more these preferences are fulfilled. Second, they have the liberty to cast their votes as they wish, in the attempt to maximize their own benefits. Third, the electoral system operates as a free market, producing the most efficient outcome, in this case the government formed from the party (or parties) whose manifesto promises the maximum collective satisfaction to the majority.

It is only relatively recently that representative democracy has achieved its fullest form, in those countries where the franchise has been extended to all adults of the appropriate nationality. Universal suffrage recognizes governmental authority as based on the natural equality, liberty and rights of all members of the electorate. But this highlights an antinomy that affects utilitarianism within both economics and politics. An unencumbered market clears to distribute goods and services in such a way that overall preference satisfaction is at its maximum, even if this entails overriding some people's individual welfare and thus violating their individual rights. The collectively optimal outcome might be sub-optimal at the individual level. The implications of this antinomy will be explored shortly.

A parallel utilitarian model applied to social relations is the rational choice or rational action approach (Coleman, 1990). The central claim of rational action theorists is that people's activities are the intended or unintended outcomes of the strategic calculations they purposively make when acting in a rationally self-interested manner, given their private preferences and their resources. Rational action theorists aim to model the structure of interdependencies between actors in order to demonstrate how their individual choices, freely made, jointly determine collective outcomes. This echoes the neoclassical micro-economics model, with the difference that individual preferences are usually taken as given by economists but are seen as the outcome of social forces by sociologists. Whereas economists examine how preferences determine behaviour which in turn produces a whole system in equilibrium, rational action sociologists examine how systems of interdependency determine individuals' preferences, which in turn generate their behaviour. Nevertheless, there is substantial overlap between the work of rational action sociologists and the tradition in economics that takes rational calculation to be the general organizing principle of social life, and extends economic analysis to non-economic transactions of all kinds (Becker, 1976). The sociology of rational action captures the modern form of civil society, comprised of the voluntary associations formed when individuals come together in the rational pursuit of their private, individual interests, unimpeded by publicly enforced arrangements purported to meet their collective needs.

There is a practical distinction between the works of economists and rational action sociologists, however. Sociologists are more prepared than economists to admit that the core assumptions of their models may need to be relaxed or expanded in order to achieve a good fit with social reality (Friedman and Hechter, 1988). These elaborations of the core rational action model are motivated by a central theme of all sociology, which is the social mediation of thought and action: people reflect their social circumstances at least to some degree. Their interdependencies mould their preferences. While still formally 'free' in the liberal sense that individuals have sole authority over their wants, the set of wants from which they choose is contextually specific; it varies historically and culturally. This highlights an antinomy between the universalism of utilitarianism, according to which the free individual's economic, political and associational preferences are unaffected by any particular ties to other individuals, traditions or understandings of the good; and the particularism of the socialized person, embedded in a web of interdependencies with others which influence the formation of their preferences. The consequences of this tension will be explored below.

## The role of trust

Trust has a supportive role to play in all three of the models; it is part of the conceptual armoury of modernist analyses of the economy, the polity and the social. The place of trust can be most clearly explained with respect to the economic model. As noted above, the neoclassical analysis rests on the assumption that individuals have full information, which they need if their cost-benefit calculation of the consequences of pursuing their various preferences is to yield reliable results. In the absence of full information, the market cannot equilibrate and there will be inefficiencies in social outcomes. 'Trust' is inserted into the rational calculation of individual costs and benefits of outcomes in the cases where the calculator lacks complete information about the other agents in an exchange. Not knowing whether the other parties will deliver their side of the bargain, one goes ahead only if one *trusts* that they will. Trust, so conceived, refers to a subjective probability that bolsters incomplete information (or, more strictly, balances informational asymmetry between the parties) in order to retain the rationality of market exchanges freely entered into by all parties. Of course, if the exchange is enforced for any party, trust is unnecessary since full information about the outcome is then available.

This notion of trust is generalizable to the other two models and it can therefore be applied in the analysis of the polity and the social. In representative democracy, it plays a large part in enabling individual voters to determine which party's programme will best meet their interests. This is especially so where the government operates over a wide range of policy issues and where the periods between elections are relatively long; both circumstances which will magnify the information deficit. Similarly, in rational action sociology the information needed to apply rationally one's preferences to alternative courses of action will often be lacking, especially when one is interacting with relative strangers.

This conception of trust suffers the same problem as all factors included in utility equations, that of finding reliable measures of them independent of the outcome that they are used to explain. Just as there is a concern that economic preferences remain hidden until revealed when goods and services are bought at a certain price, that political preferences remain hidden until votes are cast, and social preferences remain hidden until social arrangements are entered into, so trust as a subjective probability has to be inferred from its behavioural consequences. There is a danger that the only evidence for the explanans is the observation of the event described by the explanandum. It might be argued, however, that this is not an issue that is specific to trust or even to utilitarianism, but one that affects all explanations that appeal to determinants beyond our direct experience.

What factors generate increased trust? Clearly, successful experience confirms one's subjective probability estimates, and so the more often one calls upon one's trust in a particular agent and has it confirmed, the more that agent warrants one's trust for future transactions. In contrast, one disconfirming experience is likely to be fatal to an agent's trust. Thus are reputations slowly built or instantly destroyed on the verification or falsification of predictions based on trust.

Trust might be transferable from one agent to another or generalizable across a body of agents within a morally dense community; this captures something of the premodern notion of honour attached to one's station. It might also capture the suggestion that trust is underpinned by common values; if all members of a collectivity embrace a given set of values, the subjective probability established through exchanges with one person may be transferable to others. But two cautions are necessary. First, the common values might be malevolent rather than beneficent, with the result that the shared subjective probability is low not high: a situation of distrust. This might be the case if, for example, the shared value were one that encourages individuals always to take advantage in their dealings with others. Second, there is a danger of circularity if common values are claimed to support trust, but then trust is proposed as the *source* of the common values. The verification of trust through a successful interaction provides evidence for shared values and it might reinforce those values, but the shared values must exist in the first place to homogenize people sufficiently to allow the generalization of trust across them. Common values are the precursor, and transfer of trust from one agent to another is the result.

An alternative approach to the question of what generates trust is found in attempts to identify some types of agent as inspiring more trust than others independent of our experience of successfully trading or interacting with them. One such type is the non-profit organization, where the non-distributional constraint (against making a profit) could be taken as evidence that one will obtain from it better value than from a profit-making organization (see Hansmann, 1980; Ortmann and Schlesinger, 1997). This is because no portion of the price will be diverted into profit that would otherwise have been devoted to enhancing the quality of goods and services. However, the absence of profit-making is no guarantee of quality, since more of the price than would have been taken in profit might be frittered away on inefficient production processes or extravagant wages or other factors. In other words, non-profit organizations are not necessarily more intrinsically trustworthy than for-profit organizations. Thus, the attempt to locate enhanced trust within the voluntary sector fails. There are no a priori grounds for assuming that voluntary agencies are more trustworthy than organizations in the private or public sectors.

Another type of agent which might be thought to generate trust is the mutual organization, in which producers are also consumers, where being a stakeholder in the organization increases the probability that one will receive good value as a consumer. However, if the organization produces more than one good or service, there is no guarantee that the particular good or service one purchases will be of good value, since part of the price might be diverted to improve the value of one or more of the other goods and services produced by the organization. This remains true whether the mutual organization is profit-making or not. It therefore appears that there is no undisputed claim that a particular type of agent warrants more trust than other types.

Given the fragile grounds for trust, relying as it does on confirming personal experiences rather than being a characteristic of organizational type, and not being generalizable across agents in heterogeneous societies, it seems prudent to seek ways of regulating exchanges by other means in order to assure their predictability. Explicit contracts appear at first sight to offer one such means. However, mechanisms must exist through which to enforce contractual agreements, such as recourse to the laws of the state or application of professional standards. However, there is a potentially infinite regress here, as each level of agreement relies on some higher level for its enforcement. Ultimately, the infinite regress is halted by appeal to a second, generalized conception of trust. This is the tacit agreement to be bound, the implicit commitment to fair dealing, the blind trust that cannot be captured explicitly in any contract or regulation but which underpins the very notion of contract itself and even the concept of exchange or interaction more widely. It is Durkheim's 'non-contractual element of contract' (Durkheim, 1964). This second conception of trust derives from a view of people as essentially social beings. On this view, it is not relevant to conceive a 'state of nature' in which people are isolated individuals faced with the task of devising ways to form co-operative groups. Rather, everyone is born into a collectivity and part of the notion of being human involves the capacity to function in a social group, sharing at least to a minimal degree common frames of meaning that make sense of its members' activities.

This second conception of trust underpins all our dealings – economic, political and social – with our fellow social beings. It is not reliant on subscribing to a set of common values; its hold is deeper than that. It is a precondition for social engagement. And it highlights a central failing of the utilitarian agenda: if the analysis of social activity is founded on individual calculation, there is no uncontested mechanism by which to engineer social integration. Or, to cast that another way, utilitarian analyses rely implicitly on the second notion of trust, otherwise markets could not clear, even in principle.

## Charity through history

Considering the nature of trust and the bases of sociability leads on to debates about charity. Significant variations in the notion of charity can be traced through the same historical period considered at the beginning of this chapter. In Western contexts, Christian views prevailed in various forms up to the early modern period. Central here was the Augustinian belief that divine grace imparts love of God. Loving God creates the desire among the chosen to do as God commands. What He bids is to undertake worthy deeds while on earth. Most important among these is to love one's neighbour; in effect – since everyone is in principle one's neighbour – to love all of humankind. Thus true virtue derives not from pursuing one's own fulfilment and happiness on earth or in heaven but from the desire to serve God and therefore serve others, all people at all times. Universal love, or charity, is to be expressed by supporting the needy, by transferring property to them. Property is assigned to its possessors by God so that they can carry out His purposes on earth. Stewardship by the rich of God's property involves responsibility to give to the poor, the propertyless, what they need.

Interestingly, already in the twelfth century a distinction between two interpretations of charity had emerged, a distinction which still has force today (Roberts, 1996). One was an inclusive 'evangelical' view based on individuals' recognition of their spiritual responsibilities to all of the needy. But others criticized this view as indiscriminate because it ignored variations among the poor. A second, 'discriminating' view, drew distinctions among the needy, with some among them having greater call than others on God's property. This highlights the central dilemma of poor relief, whether it should be available to all in need or whether it should be deployed to discipline those among the poor who are deemed to have undesirable lifestyles. In support of the discriminating view of charity, canon lawyers drew up lists of priorities, with the righteous to be assisted before the wicked, and the wilfully idle identified as particularly undeserving. Similar attempts to divide the deserving from the undeserving poor have pervaded discussions of charity and welfare ever since. Current examples include the popular press's periodic orchestration of moral panics over 'welfare scroungers' and governments of the day forever fiddling with the rules of eligibility for welfare benefits.

In the seventeenth century, the same sceptical crisis that ushered in civil society in its early form of commercial society, prompted the development of theories of natural rights which aimed to provide a secure basis for moral theory (Schneewind, 1996). These natural human rights were thought to be so basic as to be immune from criticism by moral sceptics; they were held to provide an unquestionable basis from which to derive moral standards. They comprised qualities – such as the right to life – that belong to all people simply as individuals, and not through divine authority or because of their station in life or on any other grounds that were open to challenge. Natural rights were divided into two kinds. First, there existed perfect rights, which are modelled on contract and which can be specified with precision. These are enforced by justice, by the rules of law. Second, were imperfect rights, possessors of which are worthy of certain sorts of treatments – for example, the beggar is worthy of alms. Imperfect rights are imprecise and dependent not upon justice but on the rules of love, the desire to do good to others, which cannot be enforced. Nevertheless, although discretionary, it was argued in early modern times that love can be relied upon in everyday affairs. This, so it was claimed, is because imperfect rights and the rules of love may not be functionally necessary for society to operate, as are perfect rights and strict justice, but they improve existence. Works of love warm the hearts of others and generate sociability and solidarity beyond that produced by the performance of perfect duties enforced by justice.

The notion of imperfect rights treats Christian love in a naturalistic way. No longer is love of one's fellow humans a virtue only of those given the grace of God. Instead, it is a natural motive which humanizes the exercise of perfect rights and represents the fulfilment of human capacities. Natural disinterested benevolence universalizes Christian love. Nevertheless, when Christian love is put in secular terms by natural rights theorists, the impetus to benevolence is eroded and charity becomes discretionary. Moreover, the notion of imperfect rights offers no solution as to where to draw the line, if anywhere, between the deserving and the undeserving poor. Similarly, given that imperfect rights are not subject to the rules of law, should charity fail there is no recourse to justice to enforce it. It is not therefore surprising that argument ensues over whether the claims of the destitute to the property of the wealthy are unenforceable claims of charity or enforceable claims of justice. This argument has become particularly complex at the end of the twentieth century, when perfect rights have been extended from the negative, such as the right not to have one's life or property taken away forcibly, to the positive. These latter are typically asserted in declarations of universal human rights and include positive rights to minimum levels of goods and services, such as food, education and health.

By the nineteenth century, the increasing visibility of the deprivations of the urban poor prompted political theories and action addressed to the view that the needy were not simply the objects of imperfect duty, but victims of unjust economic structures. The tools of justice should be deployed in order to make adequate provision for the poor, for then there would be no need for individual charity dispensed at the discretion of the wealthy. Hard-edged utilitarianism supports this line: justice requires that property is transferred from one person to another if the latter can gain more utility from it than the former, and there is no room for charity (Ryan, 1996). The person who can make best use of the property has a perfect right to it, enforceable by justice, and is not limited to a discretionary, imperfect right dependent on the supererogatory benevolence of its current owner. This eviction of charity in favour of justice for the poor alarms many moral theorists and citizens because it infringes individual liberty; the freedom to choose whether or not to give. This infringement is particularly noticeable if government is the body that enforces the right to distribute property in the manner which maximizes collective utility; it sets the government against the individual, an anathema to liberalism. This again highlights the antinomy within utilitarianism drawn out earlier in the discussion of the neoclassical micro-economics model and the representative democracy model: maximizing the fulfilment of preferences across the collectivity might override the achievement of one or more individual's preferences. This antinomy strikes forcefully in the late twentieth century when people, at least in the West, subscribe to a more all-embracing egalitarianism than hitherto, founded on an increasingly broad range of positive rights as well as negative rights. This highlights people's common humanity across the globe and promotes an ideal of universal benevolence that has as its object the alleviation of suffering world-wide (Taylor, 1989). Yet counterposed to embracing the universal stranger is a vigorous, modernist claim to self-determination; we demand the right to fashion our lives as we will.

Once this utilitarian axiom of the calculated pursuit of self-interest is accepted, as it has been by many since the Enlightenment, attempts to recapture a universalistic role for charity – on the grounds that among people's preferences is the charitable (or altruistic) desire to improve the welfare of others – are unconvincing in so far as they give no reason why anyone should hold this particular preference after the religious impetus has gone. Utilitarianism, after all, puts preferences under the sole authority of the individual, and is silent on the specific desires that individuals might hold. Here, rational action sociology might be better placed than neoclassical micro-economics because, as already noted, while the latter tends to follow the utilitarian axioms strictly, the former is more willing to relax them and pay attention to the social conditions that might nurture particular wants and desires. However, while sociologists might proffer hypotheses as to the determinants of altruism, there is no strong empirical support for these, as any charitable fund-raiser will attest. In other words, charitable repertoires may flourish in particular forms among particular groups at particular times, but we know little about why, about what social conditions nurture them.

## Trust, charity and civil society

Post-Enlightenment history has bequeathed to modern social science the tools to construct incisive utilitarian analyses of economic, political and social activities. Within these analyses there is a clearly defined role for trust conceived as a subjective estimate of the probability that a given outcome will occur, which enables individuals to calculate rationally their best course of action in conditions of information asymmetry. To the extent that such conditions surround the majority of our actions, this form of trust will be widely deployed. However, the analytic incisiveness of utilitarianism is achieved only with a variety of costs. One is the problem of providing evidence for individual preferences, and for the extent of trust, independently of their behavioural outcomes. Another is the fragility of trust, in danger of falsification in every exchange we engage in. A third is that trust of this form can be generalized across agents only to the extent that they are homogeneous, sharing common values, so that expectations about how one agent will operate will hold also for others. Yet, at the beginning of the twenty-first century, as modernity gives way to forms of postmodernity in which people constantly remake their identities and societies become increasingly heterogeneous, prospects fade for generalizing trust on the basis of common values. In a highly differentiated society, confirmation of my trust in one agent provided by a mutually successful exchange gives little guarantee that I can have the same trust in another agent.

   A second conception of trust lies outside the utilitarian analytic framework but is an essential precondition for it, and therefore for the three utilitarian models of neoclassical micro-economics, representative democracy and rational action theories in sociology. This notion of trust calls on a view of people as necessarily embedded in collectivities, members of human communities, essentially social; and not as isolated individuals. Even if agents individually and independently calculate their right course of action on each occasion they act, as utilitarianism proposes, at a deeper level people participate in a communal morality which they necessarily share through their engagement with its other members since the moment of their birth. This concept of trust is one way of describing the cement that binds people together into a moral community; it captures people's worthiness of being relied upon by others, it is an essential condition for social association, for co-ordinated interaction. It is an essential precondition, too, for utilitarian accounts of action to work. This 'non-contractual element of contract' provides the necessary supporting background against which rational calculation of the best course of action can operate.

In respect of charity – the voluntary support of the needy – Christian views are universalistic, though even within this religious tradition it was proposed that there were degrees of deservedness. Once the notion of charity was naturalized in the wake of the moral scepticism of the Enlightenment, it lost its claim to apply universally. There do not seem to be any unquestionable grounds for claiming a natural perfect right to charity, enforceable by justice. Instead, charity is but an imperfect right, a discretionary exercise of benevolence. It may be part of a society's common values, but it is not necessarily so, since we can imagine communities which do not make a virtue of individuals' acting to improve the welfare of others. Charity is therefore a particularistic virtue, whose expression varies with the social and historical context. Thus, although charity is widely promoted in many societies, its incidence and form are variable. Attempts to enforce a particular form of charity, on the grounds that people's natural positive rights demand a more just distribution of goods and services, founder on disagreements about the nature and extent of such rights, often expressed as arguments over the degree of deservedness of various possible recipients of charity.

Looking back at the two notions of trust, neither has a special relationship with charity. As a precondition for interaction, trust underpins charitable activities in the same way that it underpins other economic, political and social relations. As a subjective probability estimate, trust facilitates individuals' rational calculation of outcomes in conditions of information asymmetry for charitable activities in the same way that it does for all their other activities. Where charity might feature differently is in the widespread public warmth it generates, however expressed – in terms of good neighbourliness or a bequest to a museum. This suggests that charity, often vaguely specified and evident in numerous manifestations, may feature as a common value in many societies. As we have seen, common values provide a basis for generalizing trust (in the sense of subjective probability assessments) across agents. Thus, if my trust in a particular charitable organization has in the past led me to donate to it, and nothing subsequently has falsified my trust in that organization, I might extend my trust in that organization to another charitable agent, in the belief that they share common values. But this pushes back the issue to establishing that they have shared values. Moreover, while agencies' sharing common values may be sufficient to transfer a trust estimate from one to another, it is not necessary. I might generate a trust assessment of the second organization independently of my trust estimate applied to the first.

The modern notion of civil society similarly does not have a *special* relationship with either of the two notions of trust or with charity. There is usually an implicit suggestion that voluntary social intercourse at the heart of civil society will generate common values around which people can mobilize opposition to economic and political excesses. Unfortunately, there is no necessity to this; empirically it is as likely that social intercourse exacerbates discord as promotes convergence. Nevertheless, if common values were strengthened and extended, they would form a sufficient though not necessary basis for generalizing trust (in the sense of probability estimates) across agents, as described above. Alongside this, one of the common values within civil society might be charity in some form. However, the particular form is contextually contingent, and it remains a discretionary particularistic virtue, however strongly or warmly encouraged, not a duty that could be enforced by the laws of the state.

Post-Enlightenment history alerts us not only to the explanatory strengths of utilitarianism, but also to its antinomies. These centre

# 8
# Critical Perspectives on Trust and Civil Society

*Natalie Fenton*

## Introduction

Notions of 'trust' have come to play a central role within debates regarding civic renewal, democratic reform and economic well-being (Gambetta, 1988; Putnam, 1993a; 1993b; 1995a; Fukuyama, 1996). While these may all be desirable ends, it is not clear that the meaning of 'trust', or the kinds of social relations the term is meant to describe, remain the same in each case. The contributions to this volume have sought to examine concepts of trust in a more specific way; exploring how these play out in particular contexts within civil society. At the same time the contributors have aimed to shed critical light on a larger conception of civil society using trust as an analytic tool. Perspectives on civil society proliferate (see Keane, 1988a; 1988b; 1998; Tester, 1992; Gellner, 1994), and it is arguable that the term functions most powerfully as an *idea* (Seligman, 1992) – a means of thinking about the limits of authority and freedom, or the nature of association. Recently, however, the concept of civil society has been taken up in a more prescriptive and programmatic way. The regularity of this term's appearance in contemporary policy literature (see Landry and Mulgan, 1995; Giddens, 1998; Blair, 1998), appears to support an argument that in much current political discourse, 'a *strong civil society* is seen as the answer to many of our problems of crime, disorder and social fragmentation' (Knight and Stokes, 1996: p. 6, emphasis in original). The nature and conditions of a 'strong civil society', and quite how it might provide an 'answer' to these very material problems, is not, however, self-evident or straightforward.

Seligman argues – in his contribution here, and elsewhere – that trust represents a relation between private individuals; one formed outside of legal or contractual frameworks, and beyond the ties of familism (Seligman, 1997). Civil society can be understood as that sphere where individuals come freely into association; where considerations of private interest encounter larger notions of altruism or common good (Seligman, 1992). From this perspective both trust and civil society involve a conception of the individual as essentially private, with moral agency and autonomy. Recent debates over public trust, and the prospects for civil society, tend to draw on a language of civic 'decline' and 'renewal' (see, for example, Putnam, 1995a; 1995b); and often link forms of civic or social renewal to the 'renewal' of a liberal or social democratic political project (Blair, 1998; Giddens, 1998; Szreter, 1998). In these contexts, perspectives on trust and civil society can be viewed as part of a rethinking and regrouping on the left in response to a social and political landscape radically altered by neo-liberal policies since the 1980s. It becomes critically important, therefore, to think about how theories of trust and civil society might be seen as displacing alternative ways of thinking on the left – especially in relation to notions of social solidarity. How far can a set of ideas associated with the emergence of modern social relations (Seligman, 1992; 1997; Gellner, 1994) provide an understanding of *late* modern social and economic conditions? If Seligman is right in arguing that liberal ideas of trust and civil society rest on certain precepts of individual autonomy and interest, how does the recent concern with these ideas fit with *neo-liberal* forms of individualization and marketization?

The discussion that follows begins to consolidate some of the thinking on trust and civil society that has been developed over previous chapters. It draws upon these ideas – as well as other perspectives on relations between civil society, the state, markets and individuals – to consider how the theorizing of trust might be critically extended. It develops an argument that, without social solidarity, the concepts of trust and civil society serve individualist or 'privatist' ends, and in essence represent no more than the 'human face' of capital to the detriment of collective interest. This thesis is examined in relation to two features of late modernity: individualization and marketization. The chapter has a particular concern with voluntary or charitable organizations, which occupy an especially complex position in relation to these issues: as incubators of civic virtue; as a model of activity promoted by neo-liberal 'reforms' to the welfare state; and as sites where non-market rationalities remain possible. However, these forms of voluntary association – while bearing much of the emphasis in both theoretical debates regarding trust and civil society, and in a range of recent political strategies – are not simply or necessarily conducive to inclusion or democracy.

## Trust, confidence and risk

Trust is described in different ways from several theoretical perspectives. As with related perspectives on 'confidence' and 'risk', approaches to trust are bound up with issues of uncertainty in social, economic and political life (see Giddens, 1994). Trust, however, can be a rather fragile way of responding to uncertainty. The debates on civil society alluded to in this volume suggest that, in a contemporary context, relations of trust are in danger of being overtaken by measures of confidence. This distinction between trust and confidence provides a first crucial step in understanding why analysis of the concept of trust can offer insights into different kinds of relations within civil society.

Zucker (1986) refers to three different kinds of trust: *characteristic-based trust*, that is tied to a person's social or cultural background; *process-based trust*, that is tied to past or present exchanges, as in reputation or gift exchanges; and *institutionally-based trust*, tied to forms of certification or legal constraints. Similarly, Anheier and Kendall (1998, p. 8) claim that in modern societies there has been a shift from 'particularist trust based on individual characteristic to trust based on process and experience, and then to more generalized institutional trust'. In this volume, Passey and Tonkiss argue that these kinds of shifts can be analysed as a move from trust relations to those of confidence (cf. Seligman, 1997). In the context of voluntary organizations, they interpret this as the difference between doing good (inspiring trust) and doing well (inspiring confidence). The civic value of trust is translated into the market value of confidence.

The distinction between trust and confidence and the different emphasis given to each at any one time are crucial markers in the shifting nature of relations in contemporary society. More narrow economic perspectives, in contrast, tend to conflate confidence with trust, and thus lose many of the defining factors that allow us to use these analytic concepts as indicators of social change. In a number of economic accounts (Anheier and Ben-Ner, 1997; Salamon and Anheier, 1998; Weisbrod, 1988; Hansmann, 1980) trust is related directly to market transactions and is deemed an act of rational choice that is necessary for an efficient system of economic exchange. Here, trust becomes a rational means of nego-tiating economic risk, based on the assumption that another actor will undertake an action that is not detrimental and may be bene-ficial to the agent in question. Collapsing trust and confidence in this way, however, can obscure the difference between economic and non-economic relationships within civil society, and the differ-ent ways in which people respond to the dominance of market values (particularly in areas felt to be somehow morally superior to the cut and thrust of the market – for example, the voluntary sector).

There is a wealth of literature seeking to explain what has been called 'risk society' (Beck, 1992; Lash *et al.*, 1996; Furedi, 1997; Franklin, 1998). This body of work rests on the basic premise that individual and public perceptions of uncertainty have increased in a late modern context – ecological, financial and economic risks seem greater or more random (see Macnaghten in this volume for a discussion of trust and risk in relation to the environment). A 'risk society' implies that we require greater confidence in those people and institutions that manage risk for us. The sheer volume of information being produced means that we need experts to inter-pret it for us. The growth of information is parallelled by the increasing numbers of people charged with communicating it, translating it, and making it useable. Public trust in them may be directly related to the amount of information they deliver (Bidault *et al.*, 1997). In Beck's influential account, the risk society thesis implies that individuals are more and more dependent 'upon insti-tutions and actors who may well be – and arguably are increasingly – alien, obscure and inaccessible' (Beck, 1992: p. 4). Many voluntary organizations generate trust by virtue of being external to the market (Gaskin and Fenton, 1997). However where business, public and voluntary sectors coexist – as in the provision of social services in a range of advanced capitalist democracies – the more professionalized and regulated the voluntary sector becomes. This closeness to other sectors, and the difficulty of distinguishing between various suppliers, results in a need for confidence indicators such as formal accountability procedures. If trust facilitates philanthropic behaviour, then risk encourages the replacement of such action by market considerations (Anheier and Kendall, 1998), resulting in the displacement of trust by confidence.

In a society obsessed with risk one can exercise caution but not choice. Choice is not possible because free and effective agency is constrained – by lack of information, by limited control and by potentially serious costs. A society where individuals are free to make rational decisions to fulfil their personal interests would not need trust to mediate forms of uncertainty and risk. But if individuals do not have the freedom to choose, if information received is incomplete or impenetrable, they are left with only the ability to exercise caution. With caution the concept of trust comes into the frame but what happens is not a re-establishment of trust based on traditional social cohesion, but a separation of trust and confidence where confidence becomes the overriding desire.

Risk requires external evidence that any potential danger of the transaction failing will be minimized. Accountability is a precursor for confidence. Confidence is the state you enter into when you assume your expectations will be met. If you are unsure about your expectations and are unable to predict your future needs you must enter into a relationship of trust. Some theorists use the term 'active trust' (trust which cannot be taken for granted on the basis of institutional relationships, but has to be actively produced and negotiated) as a defining characteristic of post-traditional society in which individuals are increasingly dependent on experts and increasingly aware of the shortcomings of guarantees such as those provided by the membership of a profession (Giddens, 1994: p. 93).

## Civil society and the 'crisis' of trust

Both Halfpenny and Herbert in this volume go to some lengths to explain normative principles of trust and charity in relation to particular socio-economic structures. If trust is reliant on varying normative principles then we should be able to trace how it has changed in relation to the changing nature of Western capitalist society. Putnam (1995a), talking about US society, argues that there has been a widespread loss of the sense of community that Tocqueville (1969) believed was central to American culture. Put simply, people do not trust each other as much as they used to – this is linked to a recoil from civic life and social ties. People belong to fewer organizations than they used to, vote less often, volunteer less and give proportionally less money to charity. At the same time, it is claimed that people who have retained a sense of trust are more likely to participate in almost all of these activities, establishing a link between a decline of trust and the fall in civic engagement (Putnam, 1995a; Putnam, 1995b; Brehm and Rahn, 1997; Uslaner, 1997).

Trusting involves making judgements about people or organizations that are strange to you. As civic engagement declines so social capital is lost. Social capital is a concept that embraces the trust, norms and networks that facilitate co-ordinated action. A number of commentators suggest that the 'skill' of trusting is developed in part through citizens associating in voluntary organizations, self-help groups, and mutual aid societies. Putnam (1995a) for example, has argued that a decline in participation erodes the kind of intermediary institution that Tocqueville saw as essential to the structure of civil society.

Putnam argues that forms of voluntary association are distinctive in their capacity to function as repositories for all sources of social capital – obligations and expectations, information potential and norms and sanctions (Putnam, 1993a: p. 89). As such they are characterized as incubators of civic virtue. He contends that democratic, non-exclusionary voluntary associations characterized by a high level of face-to-face interaction are involved in a virtuous circle in terms of trust, because they instil habits of co-operation, solidarity and public spiritedness; develop skills required for political activity; and prevent factionalism through inclusive membership. It is problematic, however, simply to assume that voluntary associations will be democratic and non-exclusionary – as Putnam and others have noted (Putnam, 1995a: p. 76; Portes and Landolt, 1996; Woolcock, 1998). Many commentators on the organized voluntary sector would debate whether it is quite so virtuous (see Passey and Tonkiss, this volume). A misplaced nostalgia for the civic life of the 1950s, as

Putnam cautions – let alone for Tocqueville's America of the 1830s – ignores the factors that shape and constrain association in an era of advanced modernity. Conceiving of trust as merely the way in which people relate to each other without an understanding of trust as a normative principle located in social, political and cultural frameworks, falls short of a critical analytical approach that could shed light on the development of contemporary society, in particular processes of marketization, individualization and globalization. As Putnam would have it, it seems reasonable to suppose that 'meeting in an electronic forum is not the equivalent of meeting in a bowling alley' (Putnam, 1995a: p. 76; 1995b). The very least we can say, in this context, is that the role of voluntary associations in the establishment, sustenance and demise of trust is problematic and should not be taken for granted.

## Solidarity and civil society

Misztal (1996) proposes that interest in the link between the concept of trust and that of civil society has emerged as a result of evidence suggesting that legal formulas of citizenship do not of themselves secure solidarity, participation and the expansion of the public sphere. With many symptoms of the decline of solidarity (the decrease in popularity of solidaristic parties, the decline in class solidarity, the collapse of communism as a viable alternative to capitalism), the renewal of civic institutions and the emergence of new social movements have been put forward as ways of constructing new identities and social bonds, and teaching new responsibilities and obligations. At the same time, Misztal points to the growing evidence of privatism, marketization and a politics based on rights rather than duties, as evidence of a shrinking public sphere. The task of protecting and promoting solidarity falls to the institutions of civil society which might offset the formalism, proceduralism and commodification of the state and market spheres.

Such an account places a distinctive emphasis on a politics and ethics of solidarity within civil society. Within more conventional theories of civil society, the concept of solidarity is frequently missing or side-lined. Wolfe for example, sees the role of civil society as maintaining a social fabric that tempers the operation of the market and the state and anchors them in a normative frame-work by creating 'realms of intimacy, trust, caring and autonomy that are different from the larger world of politics and economics' (Wolfe, 1989: p. 38). But solidarity is not mentioned. Indeed, the notion that politics and economics represent a 'larger world', together with a normative emphasis on values of 'intimacy, trust and caring' within civil society, appears to reinstate rather trad-itional distinctions between the public and private spheres. The civil realm is seen to exercise a *civilizing* influence on market and state, rather than providing a sphere where alternative forms of social solidarity and political agency might be articulated.

Habermas (1992), who developed the concept of the public sphere as a space where citizens freely and meaningfully could participate in public life, defines solidarity as

> the ability of individuals to respond to and identify with one another on the basis of mutuality and reciprocity without calcu-lating individual advantages and above all without compulsion. Solidarity involves a willingness to share the fate of the other, not as the exemplar of a category to which the self belongs but as a unique and different person. (Habermas, 1992: p. 47)

Thus solidarity implies both a private and a public sense of trust. To insist on the inclusion of solidarity resists the definition of civil society in simply individualistic or private terms. In what has become a very influential view, the positive potential of the public sphere as a site of solidarity and collective agency is realized by new social movements. These movements are held to engage in a kind of 'double politics'; aiming both to influence policy in a formal sense, and to construct new kinds of solidarity and collective iden-tity through informal political association – a bringing together of public and private responses.

The issue of solidarity can also be linked to debates around risk society. Lash and Urry (1994) suggest that the breakdown of trust in expert systems helps a critical reflexivity to develop. Giddens (1994: p. 6) talks about the 'expansion of social reflexivity' brought about by the wider availability of information which empowers individ-uals, enabling them to be far more critical of received wisdoms. However, this ignores the loss of collectivity in the move from trust to confidence. Individuals on their own are far more likely to be overwhelmed by a feeling of insecurity than to have the confidence to develop critical thought. Social movements provide a collective context for the formation of a critical politics. In this manner solidarity can be seen as central to an understanding of civil society which avoids assumptions of individualism.

The importance of trust in these civil contexts is heightened because of concern over the rapid decrease of trust in government and formal institutions. The British Social Attitudes Survey, for example, has indicated that the public has experienced a profound loss of faith in the institutions of the state. Its efficiency and morality have been questioned. Similar evidence has emerged from longitudinal research undertaken by The Henley Centre (Henley Centre, 1997). These claims are not restricted to Britain. A large-scale comparative analysis based on national surveys points to declining public trust in politicians in a range of 'mature' democracies, with the exception of The Netherlands (Putnam *et al.*, 2000). Data from the World Values Survey suggest a similar pattern in terms of public confidence in political institutions, including armed forces, legal systems, police, parliaments and state bureaucracies (ibid.).

These kinds of disengagement are particularly acute among the young (Gaskin *et al.*, 1996). British studies speak of extensive alienation of young people from society's central institutions and warn of the long term dangers this may have (Wilkinson and Mulgan, 1995). Some reports on young people and citizen service claim that this lack of engagement with social values and activities has fostered a host of social problems including crime and drug abuse (Briscoe, 1995). With the state in retreat – not simply in the neo-liberal sense but more broadly in terms of public support – civil society becomes foregrounded as an alternative arena of public trust, information and representation (for example, Cohen and Rogers, 1995). The defining characteristics which mark out voluntary organizations and campaigning movements from the state and market sectors – non-profit, responding to localized need, oriented to certain values and so on – become paramount in building relations of trust with members and with the wider public. The relationship between organizational form (the encouragement of active participation, democracy and inclusivity) and the potential for trust to develop is crucial to contemporary society and its practices.

However, the possibility of a renewal of civil society through the expansion of civil associations, especially voluntary organizations, is problematic principally because such organizations do not necessarily increase democratic inclusion or operate in a manner that inculcates trust. Notions of trust and civil society may widely be seen as providing the foundations for general social solidarity and moral community. However, without an emphasis on forms of collective identity and an active and critical sense of solidarity, the concept of civil society remains centred on the individual and their interests, rather than on mutuality or reciprocity. Most importantly, it is not clear whether this thing called civil society simply builds on an association of interest that may have arisen out of the individualization of lifestyles organized around consumption in the market-place, or whether it is based on something more than enlightened self-interest. This is a point that is developed below.

## Why does trust have particular relevance to contemporary society?

### Individualization

Neo-liberalism, based on an ideology of economically centred individualism, consumerism and citizenship, held sway in a range of liberal capitalist governments throughout the 1980s and 1990s – most notably in the United Kingdom and the United States. In the UK, Thatcherism was described as the only 'political and moral force that has been in the business of eating away at the cement of social reciprocity' (Hall, 1993: p. 14). Neo-liberal policies have been blamed widely for undermining the welfare state and eroding social solidarity, including the responsibility that people may feel for one another. As the consequences of pushing market principles to the limit became apparent political support was mobilized by recourse to such popular themes as crime, family breakdown and social disintegration, allowing a nostalgia for community and social cohesion to fill the void.

The concept of active citizenship or citizen participation also resonates with a very different ideology that emerged from the 1960s and 1970s in the UK of participatory democracy in service planning and delivery. There is a huge gulf between these two ideologies that the introduction of the concept of communitarianism tried to bridge. Communitarianism relies on the values and frameworks put in place by forms of voluntary association (Etzioni, 1993). In a formal sense, civil society is frequently claimed to be built on the health of non-governmental, non-market organizations – this notion of the third sector is a cornerstone of the vision of the New Labour government in the United Kingdom (the so-called 'third way'). Voluntarism is central to Labour's neo-liberal policies. If the third sector cannot be carried to new levels of social innovation and provision for unmet social need, then Blair's third way is unlikely to become a reality.

However, despite the recent compact on relations between government and the voluntary and community sector (HMSO, 1998) that declares the independence of non-governmental organizations from government, the need for consistent funding policies, the right to consultation on future policy documents and the need for improved accountability procedures, charitable giving and volunteering are not generally increasing. This would seem to point to the fact that charitable giving and a spirit of voluntarism are motivated by more than just sympathetic social policy; rather, they are shaped by a particular socio-economic history that has promoted certain ideologies that do not disappear on demand.

The growth of individualism and the breakdown of community in the UK have been linked to the Conservative government's long term in power and also used to explain the decline of trust. Commentators have remarked that the rise of individualism, especially in the 1980s, has been at the expense of sociability and civic-mindedness. Such arguments are based on the assumption that if individual self-interest is allowed to develop unhindered, conflicts of interests will override relations of trust. These ideas are not exactly new. Durkheim (1957; 1968) argued that a society composed of isolated individuals pursuing their own narrow objectives was untenable. According to Durkheim, calculating individuals pursuing their own self interest undermined social solidarity. To overcome this danger society required a morality of co-operation and a network of secondary institutions which bound people together – these would help to mediate the pursuit of self interest by creating social bonds (Furedi, 1997).

The 1980s saw the New Right attempt to remove limitations on the accumulation and power of capital in the market-place. Their project was to roll back the priorities of the social democratic state with its commitment to welfare, full employment and 'high' taxation to fund these. The role of the state would instead be to remove restrictions on the free market in labour (unions, wages policies and so on), to deregulate and allow larger units of capital to form (to increase profitability) and to reward the wealth-makers. To do this governments reduced direct taxation to allow the market to develop in an unfettered and global fashion (Philo and Miller, 1997).

Policy analysts (such as Le Grand, 1997; Taylor-Gooby, 1999) have argued that these shifts from social democracy to neo-liberalism, and the policies accompanying them, are underpinned by particular assumptions regarding human motivation (Le Grand, 1997). Le Grand distinguishes three 'types' of social actor, each delimited in terms of their motivations. A social democratic model of 'knights' and 'pawns', as he has it, has been increasingly displaced by 'knavish' motivations. In the former model, those who financed and operated state welfare systems were predominantly public-spirited or altruistic in motivation (knights), and users of welfare services were essentially passive or unresponsive recipients of state largesse (pawns). However, this model has been supplanted by more 'knavish' motivations, wherein individuals are essentially motivated by self-interest. The reported unwillingness of citizens to pay more tax, ongoing scares over 'dole-cheats', and 'workfare' initiatives (especially in the US and the UK) are examples of how this model of motivation might shape various policy arenas.

Taylor-Gooby (1999), similarly, considers the motivations behind particular courses of action. The assumption is that an understanding of the motives behind peoples' actions can aid a wider understanding of society, how stability is reached, and processes of social change. Rationality is forwarded as one explanation typical of economic models of human behaviour. Many sociologists, however, argue that political ideologies and cultural frameworks create particular conditions that are conducive to certain ways of thinking – normative principles that transcend simple rationality. The problem of sustaining trust in a market system falls prey to both arguments. As Taylor-Gooby puts it: '[t]he risk is that over-reliance on a rational choice account of motivation in welfare markets may lead to over-emphasis on self-interest which will eventually deplete the normative legacy of welfare citizenship' (1999: p. 99). If we allow the concept of social good to develop on the basis of a rational choice model we effectively hand it over to the principles of the market.

The emergence of global markets produces key changes to relationships in society (Waters, 1995; Featherstone, 1990). The market is far more than simply the mechanism through which demands are met. It is itself a system of values and relationships. At an interpersonal level these are manifest, at least in part, as competitive struggle between individuals.

## Marketization

In a market society individual status is conferred by the ability to buy, to demand service and thus to control others. The key commodity in such a society is human labour. People compete to sell and market themselves and the individual struggle for success can undermine collectivist and social responses. Personal success is measured by individual market-value. The outward expression of new forms of market dominance can be seen in practices of consumption. The ability to consume becomes a marker of individual rights and social relations of power (Philo and Miller, 1997). These values are not new, but are offered in a more developed and legitimized form in contemporary Western societies. The new prominence of these values has been contested by social alternatives from the left, and by moralism from the right. Against these currents, the values of the market celebrate a social and material world which is for sale and is thereby reduced to a mass of commodities. The common exchange relationship is predicated on purchasing power. Making a purchase involves a legal contract whereby the consumer can exercise their rights to acceptable consumption. Such is the power of the market that individual rights overwhelm social rights based on a notion of collective good that may or may not be to the advantage of the individual.

In turn, relations between individuals are increasingly governed by economic forces. Public support for charities, for example, often assumed to be an altruistic act, has not escaped the individualization of the market. The social response to charitable giving relies frequently on assessments of deservedness of the beneficiary. Perceptions of who receives charity and who should receive charity are linked to the willingness of people to support charities (Fenton *et al.*, 1993). Public attitudes on the seeming excess of voluntary and charitable organizations operating in the same field and the high administrative costs such organizations incur are common (Fenton *et al.*, 1995). But more than this, the recipients of charity themselves are often viewed with nothing more than contempt, malign distrust or corrosive pity (Golding and Middleton, 1982). A society so firmly entrenched in an ethic of competition and reward finds it difficult to escape the values it espouses.

However, public attitudes do not always obediently follow the wholesale promotion of the market. Individualism and consumerism have not gone unquestioned by the public. Other attitudes prevail that mark civil society as different in character from both the state and the world of business. For example, voluntary organizations are perceived as offering an opportunity to somehow defy the market and act on principles other than profit and power. In the UK, research has shown that the ability of voluntary organizations to represent something other than the market is vital to their future well-being (Gaskin and Fenton, 1997).

The contradictory responses that the voluntary sector provokes can be explained by reference to the particular history of the welfare state in Britain: the Conservative ethos of consumption and citizen participation (often referred to as individual citizenship) was built on a prior history of participatory democracy and social citizenship. As Taylor and Lansley (1992) point out, both involve a shift away from paternalism, whether of the ruling elite or the 'nanny state' and towards a greater choice of services whether on an individual or communal basis. They suggest that the 'consumerist individual whose personal choices create aggregate demand for market pluralism may thus overlap with the citizen, who is drawn into the collective action of welfare pluralism' (Taylor and Lansley, 1992: p. 172). The consumerist individual has their sights on the market, the citizen has their sights on moral and social rights.

Furedi (1997) takes individualism one step further, linking marketization of society to a process of 'individuation' – as opposed to the promotion of individualism – that is directly related to the erosion of relations of trust. It has become fashionable to describe society today as one which is uniquely 'individual' but this denies significant anti-individual strands that are prevalent in a range of social contexts. For example, it has become common to criticize those on high salaries and those who indulge in conspicuous consumption. These criticisms are particularly salient when directed towards voluntary organizations. The salaries of directors are questioned for being too competitive; fundraising is deemed to be too professional and thus too expensive.

Furedi (1997) argues that such themes are sustained by a philosophy of caution and scepticism which criticizes those who go too far and thereby put others at risk – the viciousness of modernity is recognized but any alternative is not. Where scepticism towards the market is expressed by way of hostility to certain actors within it, this is not – in Furedi's argument – a liberating reaction; rather it increases individualism and the weakening of solidarity. Individuation operates in a culture of distrust, cynicism and fear. This highlights the difficulty of translating the concept of individual citizenship to one of social rights: '[g]roups and individuals, their demands and needs cannot be reduced to a simple formula' (Cochrane, 1998: p. 262). To recognize the perils of the market and attempt to keep it within limits ensures that the market is managed and individualism is never fully challenged.

These arguments have particular implications for charities and other forms of voluntary organization. Charity is seen as both helping those in difficulties and providing a mechanism through which caring impulses can be channelled and forms of 'social connectedness' (Putnam, 1995b) established. The charitable and civic spirit has therefore both individual and social elements that can be exercised by way of voluntary organizations. On the other hand clear scepticism is expressed about the reasons for the continued existence of so many charities operating in a competitive market place (Gaskin and Fenton, 1997). This is an expression of a particular history of individual and social citizenship. Social capital previously accumulated is not easily dissolved and may be re-invoked but it does so in an environment dominated by the market and individuation – what is referred to above as 'vicious modernity'. If we are to accept that traditional conceptions of trust and civil society have relevance in a contemporary context, then we must first and foremost accept that the lived experience of 'trust' or 'citizenship' emanates from particular social histories. It may be that the global market place has been resoundingly successful in propagating ideologies of individualism and consumerism where they have the conditions and freedom to flourish (most noticeably in the Western developed world), but they do so among histories that are also drenched in other ideologies, more commonly associated with solidarity, that potentially conflict with market values.

Individualization foregrounds choice as the ultimate act of freedom and sign of democracy. However, choice is a fluid, complex and socially conditioned process. Any act of decision-making is influenced by circumstances. Individuals can not be assumed to have access to a stable and consistent set of preferences to refer to in making decisions. Herbert and Halfpenny (this volume) illustrate how trust is fundamentally tied to particular socio-economic structures. While large-scale processes of market-ization and individualization may be seen as transforming the basis of trust and the meaning of citizenship on a broad scale, it is important to also consider more local factors that may exert a powerful influence on how such notions are understood.

## Local politics in global structures

If the free market policies of neo-liberal governments promoted forms of competitive individualism, they may also be seen to have weakened community structures. The uneven development of the capitalist market plus its tendency to rapid expansion and contraction has historically put pressure on local community structures, particularly by forcing the movement or displacement of labour. The expansion of the market tends to change both individual relationships and corporate priorities. There are many different social responses to this. Some of these are based on traditional forms of collectivism, as evident in a recent growth in trade unionism in the United States. There has also been a growth of local struggles over road-building, animal rights, ethnic or cultural identities which indicate the development of new forms of cultural resistance. Research in the UK has revealed that there is general support for the involvement of charities in lobbying and campaigning – the product of a social democratic history. But more emphatically expressed is a preference for *local* charities. This preference relates to the opportunity to see the results of the voluntary organization's action, and its impact on the individual's local community and also because it usually implies a small-scale initiative that is more readily accountable (Gaskin and Fenton, 1997). The demand for accountability can be seen as the product of a market system that requires confidence in the exchange relationship it relies upon.

The affinity with local charities, or national charities which have local programmes, is related to the supporter's sense of connection and control (see Macnaghten, this volume). Once distance, and all the mediating mechanisms between handing over one's donation and its arrival as food in the mouth of a starving child are considered, greater confidence is expressed that a local or domestic donation is more likely to be of real benefit to its intended recipient (Gaskin and Fenton, 1997). There is general suspicion that sheer size might work against effectiveness. A large organization is seen as more likely to contain excessive bureaucracy and have too many administrators (that is, be too like the state); or be too professionalized (mimicking techniques of business that are deemed unsuitable for the voluntary sector). Voluntarism, whether through the giving of time or money, depends heavily on a sense of trust which reflects a basic sense of optimism and control. On a local level, people's proximity to the activities of the organization, as well as concepts of community, belonging and duty, combine to make trust an active ingredient of voluntarism. The distance of these organizations from market imperatives of profit also make trust relations more viable.

James (1987) argues that certain voluntary organizations that act on a religious, political or ideological basis, or are oriented to specific client groups, create 'captive audiences'. In guiding these audiences through part of their social life, voluntary organizations contribute to the development of values and beliefs. In this manner voluntary organizations provide more or less implicit information on whom to trust and whom not to trust. While the localization of political struggle which forges communities and often pitches them against larger or more distant corporations can operate contrary to a global market logic, it also falls prey to the same criticisms. A lack of central co-ordination between organizations may be perceived negatively by the public, resulting in confusion about the size and scope of the sector (Gaskin and Fenton, 1997). Without central co-ordination the growth in charities is perceived as increased competition between organizations working for the same or similar causes. Thereby voluntary organizations fall foul of the criticisms of the market on two contradictory accounts: for being too localized or individual in their response; and for competing against potential allies and being too global, out of touch, inefficient and wasteful.

There is a further problem for voluntary organizations that are drawn into the world of local politics through the provision of social services once provided by the state. These organizations tread a difficult path between satisfying the demand of those who issue the contracts (local or central government authorities) and the demands of their members or those they seek to represent. There is a tension between accepting the rules of the more powerful partner, to ensure that resources are made available for activities that are befitting of the aims of the voluntary organization, and losing touch with the members or supporters of those organizations. This is particularly the case when levels of participation begin to dwindle as the work of organizations becomes routinized and professionalized (Cochrane, 1986). In these cases solidarity is more difficult to uphold as the organization is seen to mimic the techniques and practices of the private or statutory sectors, relations of confidence step in and accountability procedures take over. The spirit of voluntarism, or what was earlier referred to as mutuality and reciprocity, is lost.

Localization of political struggle is paralleled by a fragmentation of political culture in which party allegiances and class alliances give way to more fluid and informal networks of action. Such networks are often staunchly anti-bureaucratic and anti-centralist, suspicious of large organized, formal and institutional politics. In turn, the fragmentation of political culture is fuelled by the rise of identity politics in which modern logics of incorporation and representation are challenged on the bases of their rigidity and exclusiveness. In contrast, the recognition of local diversity allows for differentiated notions of citizenship in alternative public spheres. Any workable notion of civil society depends on the possibility of a continuing process of renewal, in which there is always access to emerging organizations or new ones that can be created and recognized relatively easily.

Trust is engendered most readily through proximity, not only geographically but also personally. The most trusted sources of information on charities are friends and family. This personal trust in the private sphere overlaps with social trust in the public sphere. Gaskin and Fenton (1997) point out that in the Langford and

McDonald (1997) study non-governmental, campaign-driven organizations had a high trust rating because many people believed
such campaigns were conducted in the public interest and targeted
against institutions that cannot be relied upon. In this context, how
accountability is practised and understood is central to levels of
trust and confidence in the voluntary sector. Johnson *et al.* (1998)
argue that trust is an essential element of quality assurance in the
voluntary sector. But trust relies on taking charities on their word;
accountability requires a process of standards, measurement and
audit that can systematically encourage confidence through information provision – the translation of civic values into market
values.

The ability of voluntary organizations to inform the public about
their work has been dramatically affected by instantaneous commu-
nications technologies. Together with patterns of mass migration
and world trade new technologies increase awareness of, and
dependence between, localities far away from each other. This can
be seen as positive in so far as it can raise awareness of the politics
of consumption – as Giddens (1990) notes the choices and actions
of consumers in one locality can have an impact on the international division of labour and planetary ecology. Large international
voluntary organizations can and do inform the public of the impact
of a global economy. But it is a function that often precludes participation and negates any degree of control on behalf of the giver.
Such groups may have large memberships but the members rarely,
if ever, see one another. People may be committed givers but the
giving is organized at a distance, the act of participation is at arm's
length. Solidarity is qualified. Altruism is relegated to a financial
relationship. Neither trust nor confidence can easily flourish.

## Conclusion

Contemporary Western societies are characterized by processes of
marketization, individualization and globalization. These developments have grown out of social histories that are not always
consistent and sometimes directly at odds with the values of a
market society. At the same time, relations of trust, where and if
they existed before, appear to have been eroded or at least to have
been invaded by complexity and cynicism. Trust itself may still be

seen as an admirable aim – a desired state of being – but the means
of attaining it are muddied by the values of a system that pitches
against it. If we believe that trust is somehow a fundamental precursor for social capital, and that civil society is the pre-eminent site
for the development of trust, then a neo-liberal agenda that priori-
tizes the narrow interests of capital and foregrounds the importance
of markets that undercut trust, threatens the nurturing of civil
society itself.

Individualism is linked directly to a free market economy which
is based on the social contract that states – I pay you for a service
that you will deliver. The exchange relationship is based on the
principles of market exchange and need never involve person to
person relations at all, as the development of the internet bears
testament. Trust is most easily gained in interactions that are
person to person. The social contract replaces social contact, resulting in the displacement of trust by confidence. The market
equivalent of a trusting relationship is accountability in a spirit of
civility. Markets rely on confidence provided through regulation.
Accountability replaces responsibility. The only thing for which
you are responsible is your part of the social contract.

Civil society is now widely accepted as a concept that will inform
and uphold democracy. Although, exactly how and by what mechanisms civil society is to be invoked is often unclear. What I have
tried to suggest in this chapter is that without solidarity, trust and
civil society are individualistic concepts and represent no more
than the human face of capitalism. On the left new solidaristic ideas
recognize the need for democratization of the state and the public
realm while accepting the demand for choice and individual rights
established within advanced capitalism. Tony Blair's attempts to
redefine the British Labour Party by stressing community, responsibility and trust, or Bill Clinton's call for a 'spirit of community' and
a politics of the common good, are both examples of democratic
communitarianism now popular on the left. However, the possibility of a renewal of solidarity through an increase in civil and
voluntary organizations is problematic because, as argued above,
such organizations do not necessarily increase democratic inclusion
or operate in a manner that inculcates trust. Instances where voluntary organizations are perceived by the public to act in a manner
more suited to the business and statutory sector are, in the main,

cases where they have taken over the role of social services previously the domain of the state. In a communitarian society it is these very roles of voluntary organizations that would be developed.

The relationship between citizen and government has become increasingly opaque in a world of multiple stakeholders, including businesses, hybrid public-private organizations, public sector agencies and individuals. It is often unclear who is accountable to whom for what, and even less clear what the relationship is between citizen and agency on many issues. As Cochrane (1998) states, particular agencies' degree of responsibility is often unclear when there are overlapping sources of subsidy, financial support and membership. This confusion and complexity works against relations of trust – and often serves to undermine levels of confidence.

A further reason why the concepts of trust and civil society should not forego the concept of solidarity is their need to embrace both the public and the private, thereby going beyond conventional models of civil society. It may be possible that trust can be generated through secondary associations which mediate between the private sphere of the family and the public sphere of the state (cf. Fukuyama, 1996: p. 62). However, as noted above, the question of whether civil society simply builds on associations of interest that may have arisen out of the individualization of lifestyles organized around consumption in the market place, or whether it is based on something more than enlightened self-interest, is crucial to further theorizing in this field. Is a 'strong civil society' something that will enhance and deepen democracy through increased participation in the public sphere, or is it rather a neo-liberal attempt at reconciling the demands of individual choice with the need for social cohesion? Hirst (1994) offers a vision of the future in which there is a substantial devolution of power down from the centralized state to a system of voluntary self-governing associations. But he also states that 'the core ethical claim of associationism ... is justified on essentially individualistic terms' (Hirst, 1994: p. 50). As Powell (this volume) argues 'trust, empathy and compassion are the common elements that transcend utilitarian individualism'. If solidarity is central to relations of trust then the continued pursuit of an individualistic response to questions of welfare is problematic. The project of re-establishing trust for the benefit of an enhanced democracy must recast the concept of civil society in this frame.

In the UK the belief in the new role of the voluntary sector as the crucible of a strong civil society has been promulgated without an explication of individual rights and entitlements to various services, without defining the concept of 'voluntary' or 'needy', without considering possible conflicts between professional and non-professional personnel, and without due consideration to the advocacy, campaigning and monitoring work that is the *raison d'être* of many organizations within this sphere. Ideological concepts of citizenship, consumerism and participation exist side by side in contradictory and confused relationships and have become part of people's various understandings of the meaning and purpose of 'charity' (see Gaskin and Fenton, 1997, for example, for a discussion of hardening public attitudes towards homelessness).

The concept of trust is bound up with complex questions of consumption, regulation and representation. It is a personal response to a social dilemma that characterizes contemporary Western society – the dilemma of the consumer and the citizen, of the individual and society, of the local and the global. As Sztompka (1998b: p. 25) argues, 'any existing measure of trust is path-dependent; its meaning, strength, durability, the direction of future evolution depend to a large extent on its origins'. The argument in this chapter suggests that we exist in an era of modernity where the market constitutes a system of values that is closely linked to the development not only of public attitudes, but also to people's willingness to make donations of time or money, and their propensity for civic engagement. In this context, the development of trust relations within forms of civil and voluntary association is problematic. Recourse to classical models of trust, based on interactions between free, rational and private individuals, is insufficient to late modern social conditions. In a society characterized by individualization and marketization, increasing uncertainty and perceptions of risk, the art of trusting has become a complex process.

As Woldring (1998: p. 371) notes, Tocqueville, as an early contributor to debates over civil society, recognized that new social policies 'can not succeed till certain changes in the conditions, customs and mental habits of men have prepared a way for their reception' (Tocqueville, 1988: p. 11). Without such a foundation as a basis for support, a democratic government is not able legitimately to pursue its policy of intervention. Social structures condition and change patterns of thought, customs and values. The concept of civil society and the concept of trust are a result of both the social, political and economic frameworks from which they have arisen, and the contingent and complex ways in which they operate today. Recent strategies, on both the left and the right, to mark out civil society as an extended sphere of welfare provision and social regulation – and to invoke an ill-defined notion of 'trust' as a basis for wider social cohesion – come into conflict with alternative visions of civil society as a site for critical and diverse forms of solidarity. If conventional distinctions between civil society and the state have been discredited of late, this is in part due to the manner in which actors and organizations within the 'civil' sphere have been integrated into neo-liberal strategies of government (see Rose, 1996). Normative models of civil society, then, are not only objects of theoretical speculation, but underpin the instrumental version of civil society that animates current policy discourses and welfare reforms. The chapters in this volume suggest that we should proceed with caution and trust not.

# Bibliography

Abrams, M. *et al.* (1985) *Values and Social Change in Britain.* London: Macmillan.

Adam, B. (1995) *Timewatch.* Cambridge: Polity.

Alexander, J. C. (1998) *Real Civil Societies: Dilemmas of Institutionalization.* London: Sage.

Ali, Y. (1992) 'Muslim Women and the Politics of Ethnicity in Northern England', in G. Saghal and N. Yuval-Davis (eds), *Refusing Holy Orders: Women and Fundamentalism in Britain.* London: Virago.

Anderson, A. (1997) *Media, Culture and the Environment.* London: UCL Press.

Anderson, D. (1996) 'Bringing Civil Society to an Uncivilised Place', in C. Haunt and E. Dunne (eds), *Civil Society.* London: Routledge.

Anheier, H. K. and Ben-Ner, A. (1997) 'Shifting Boundaries: Long-term Changes in the Size of the For-profit, Non-profit and Co-operative and Government Sectors', *Annals of Public and Co-operative Economics,* 68/3.

Anheier, H. K. and Kendall, J. (1998) 'Trust, Voluntarism and Non-profit Organizations: Theoretical Perspectives'. Unpublished paper.

Antov, N. and Nash, J. (1999) 'Islamic Civil Society in Turkey.' Unpublished paper presented at *Islam and Human Rights in Post-Communist Europe,* Sofia, 15–16 March.

Atal, Y. (1999) *Poverty in Transition and Transition in Poverty.* New York: UNESCO/Berghahn.

Attiyah, P. S. (1979) *The Rise and Fall of the Freedom of Contract.* Oxford: Clarendon Press.

Avineri, S. (1981) *The Making of Modern Zionism: The Intellectual Origins of the Jewish State.* New York: Basic Books.

Banks, J. and Tanner, S. (1997) *The State of Donation: Household Gifts to Charity 1974–1996.* London: Institute for Fiscal Studies.

Baron, J. and Hannon, M. (1994) 'The Impact of Economics on Contemporary Sociology', *Journal of Economic Literature* 32: 1111–46.

Beck, U. (1992) *Risk Society: Towards a New Modernity.* London: Sage.

Beck, U. (1996) 'World Risk Society as Cosmopolitan Society?', *Theory, Culture and Society* 13: 1–32.

Becker, G. (1976) *The Economic Approach to Human Behaviour.* Chicago: University of Chicago Press.

Becker, M. B. (1994) *The Emergence of Civil Society in the Eighteenth Century.* Bloomington: Indiana University Press.

Bell, D. (1989) 'American Exceptionalism Revisited: The Role of Civil Society', *The Public Interest* 95: 38–56.

Berking, H. (1996) 'Solidary Individualism', in S. Lash, B. Szerszynski and B. Wynne (eds), *Risk, Environment and Modernity.* London: Sage.

174

Beyer, P. (1994) *Religion and Globalization*. London: Sage.

Bidault, F., Gomez, P. and Marion, G. (1997) *Trust: Firm and Society*. London: Macmillan.

Blackburn, R. (ed.) (1991) *After the Fall*. London: Verso.

Blair, T. (1998) *The Third Way: New Politics for a New Century*. London: Fabian Society.

Bourdieu, P. (1984) *Distinction: A Social Critique of the Judgment of Taste*. Cambridge, MA: Harvard University Press.

Bourdieu, P. (1986) 'The Forms of Capital', in J. G. Richardson (ed.), *Handbook of Theory and Research for the Sociology of Education*. New York: Greenwood Press.

Bourdieu, P. and Passeron, J-C. (1990) [1970] *Reproduction in Education, Society and Culture*. London: Sage.

Bourdieu, P. and Wacquant, L. (1992) *Invitation to Reflexive Sociology*. Chicago: University of Chicago Press.

Boyle, D. (1999) 'Time is a Great Social Healer', *New Statesman* 23 Aug. 18–20.

Brehm, J. and Rahn, W. (1997) 'Individual Level Evidence for the Causes and Consequences of Social Capital', *American Journal of Political Science* 41: 888–1023.

Briscoe, I. (1995) *In Whose Service? Making Community Service Work for the Unemployed*. London: Demos.

Britton, N. J. and Davis Smith, J. (1999) 'Recruiting and Retaining Black Volunteers: A Study of a Black Voluntary Organisation', *Voluntary Action* 1/3: 9–23.

Bryson, L. (1992) *The Middle Classes and the Welfare State: Who Benefits?* London: Macmillan.

Burchell, G., Gordon, C. and Miller, P. (eds) (1991) *The Foucault Effect: Studies in Governmentality*. Hemel Hempstead: Harvester Wheatsheaf.

Burke, T. (1997) 'The Buck Stops Everywhere', *New Statesman*, 20 June.

Calhoun, C. (ed.) (1993) *Habermas and the Public Sphere*. Cambridge, MA: MIT Press.

Cantrell, B. and Kemp, U. (1993) 'The Role of the Protestant Churches in Eastern Germany: Some Personal Experiences and Reflections', *Religion, State and Society*, 21/2–3: 277–88.

Cantwell Smith, W. (1998) *Faith and Belief: The Difference Between Them*. London: One World.

Carmen, R. (1990) *Communication, Education & Empowerment*. Manchester: Manchester University Press.

Casanova, J. (1994) *Public Religions in the Modern World*. Chicago: Chicago University Press.

Castells, M. (1996) *The Rise of the Network Society*. Oxford: Blackwell.

Castells, M. (1997a) *The Power of Identity*. Oxford: Blackwell.

Castells, M. (1997b) *End of Millennium*. Oxford: Blackwell.

CEC (1995) *Europeans and the Environment in 1995: Eurobarometer 43.1*. Brussels: European Commission.

Chomsky, N. (1996) *Class Warfare*. London: Pluto Press.

Coase, R. (1937) 'The Nature of the Firm', *Economica* 4: 386–405.

Coase, R. (1960) 'The Problem of Social Cost', *Journal of Law and Economics* 3: 1–44.

Coase, R. (1984) 'The New Institutional Economics', *Journal of Law and Economics* 27: 229–31.

Cochrane, A. (1986) 'Community Politics and Democracy', in D. Held and C. Pollitt (eds), *New Forms of Democracy*. London: Sage.

Cochrane, A. (1998) 'Globalisation, Fragmentation and Local Welfare Citizenship', in J. Carter (ed.), *Postmodernity and the Fragmentation of Welfare*. London: Routledge.

Cohen, E. (1983) 'Ethnicity and Legitimation in Contemporary Israel', *Jerusalem Quarterly* 28: 111–24.

Cohen, J. and Arato, A. (1992) *Civil Society and Political Theory*. Cambridge, MA: MIT Press.

Cohen, J. and Rogers, J. (eds) (1995) *Associations and Democracy*. London: Verso.

Coleman, J. (1987) *Individual Interests and Collective Action*. Cambridge: Cambridge University Press.

Coleman, J. (1988) 'Social Capital in the Creation of Human Capital', *American Journal of Sociology* 94: S95–S120.

Coleman, J. (1990) *Foundations of Social Theory*. Cambridge, MA: Harvard University Press.

Comité des Sages (1996) *Report by the Comité des Sages for a Europe of Civil and Social Rights*. Luxembourg: European Commission.

Commission on Social Justice (1994) *Social Justice: Strategies for National Renewal*. London: Vintage.

Cooper, T. (1991) *An Ethic of Citizenship for Public Administration*. Englewood Cliffs, NJ: Prentice-Hall.

Crawford, B. (ed.) (1995) *States, Markets and Democracy: The Political Economy of Post-Communist Transition*. Boulder: Westview Press.

Dahrendorf, R. (1990) *Betrachtungen uber die Revolution in Europa*. Stuttgart: Deutsche Verlag-Anstalt.

Darcy de Oliveira, M. and Tandon, R. (1994) *Citizens: Strengthening Global Civil Society*. Washington: Civicus.

Davis Smith, J. (1998a) 'Making a Difference: Can Governments Influence Volunteering?', *Voluntary Action* 1/1: 7–20.

Davis Smith, J. (1998b) *The 1997 National Survey of Volunteering*. London: Institute for Volunteering Research.

Deakin, N. (1996) *Meeting the Challenge of Change: Voluntary Action into the 21st Century*. Report of the Commission on the Future of the [UK] Voluntary Sector. London: National Council for Voluntary Organisations.

De Gruchy, J. (1995) *Christianity and Democracy*. Cambridge: Cambridge University Press.

Department of the Environment [DoE] (1994) *Digest of Environmental Protection and Water Statistics*, No. 16. London: HMSO.

Donzelot, J. (1991) 'The Mobilization of Society', in G. Burchell, C. Gordon and P. Miller (eds), *The Foucault Effect: Studies in Governmentality*. Hemel Hempstead: Harvester Wheatsheaf.

Downs, A. (1957) *An Economic Theory of Democracy*. New York: Harper & Row.

Durkheim, E. (1957) *Professional Ethics and Civil Morals*. London: Routledge.

Durkheim, E. (1964) *The Division of Labour in Society*. New York: Free Press.

Durkheim, E. (1968) *Sociology and Philosophy*. New York: Free Press.

Durkheim, E. (1973) *Emile Durkheim on Morality and Society*. Chicago: Chicago University Press.

Dwyer, K. (1991) *Arab Voices: The Human Rights Debate in the Middle East*. London: Routledge.

Eisenstadt, S. N. (1956) 'Ritualized Personal Relations', *Man* 56: 90-95.

Eisenstadt, S. N. (1985) *The Transformation of Israeli Society*. Boulder: Westview Press.

Elias, N. (1982) *The Civilizing Process*. New York: Pantheon Books.

Esposito, J. (1991) *Islam: The Straight Path*. Oxford: Oxford University Press.

Etzioni, A. (1988) *The Moral Dimension: Towards a New Economics*. New York: Free Press.

Etzioni, A. (1993) *The Spirit of Community: Rights, Responsibilities and the Communitarian Agenda*. New York: Crown.

Everett, W. (1997) *Religion, Federalism and the Struggle for Public Life*. Oxford: Oxford University Press.

Featherstone, M. (ed.) (1990) *Global Culture*. London: Sage.

Feirabend, J. and Rath, J. (1996) 'Making a Place for Islam in Politics', in W. Shadid and S. van Koningsveld (eds), *Muslims in the Margin: Political Response to the Presence of Islam in Western Europe*. Kampen: Kok Pharos.

Fenton, N., Golding, P. and Radley, A. (1993) *Charities, Media and Public Opinion*. Loughborough University: Department of Social Sciences.

Fenton, N., Golding, P. and Radley, A. (1995) 'Charities, Media and Public Opinion', *Research Bulletin*, Winter 1995, 37: 10–15. London: HMSO.

Ferguson, A. (1782) [1767] *An Essay on the History of Civil Society*. London: T. Cadell.

Ferris, J. M. (1998) 'The Role of the Nonprofit Sector in a Self-governing Society: A View from the United States', *Voluntas* 9/2: 137–51.

Fischer, S. (1996) 'Hahareidim miehashalom', *Theory and Criticism* 9 (in Hebrew).

Fischer, S. (1999) 'Lamah Shas', *Theory and Criticism* 12 (in Hebrew).

Foucault, M. (1979) *Discipline and Punish*. London: Penguin.

Franklin, J. (ed.) (1998) *The Politics of the Risk Society*. Cambridge: Polity.

Friedman, D. and Hechter, M. (1988) 'The Contribution of Rational Choice Theory to Macrosociological Research', *Sociological Theory* 6: 201–18.

Fukuyama, F. (1996) *Trust: The Social Virtues and the Creation of Prosperity*. London: Penguin.

Fukuyama, F. (1999) *The Great Disruption: Human Nature and the Reconstitution of Social Order*. London: Profile.

Furedi, F. (1997) *Culture of Fear: Risk-taking and the Morality of Low Expectation*. London: Cassell.

Galtung, J. (1994) *Human Rights in Another Key*. Cambridge: Polity.

Gambetta, D. (ed.) (1988) *Trust: Making and Breaking Co-operative Relations*. Oxford: Basil Blackwell.

Gaskin, K. and Dobson, B. (1996) *The Economic Equation of Volunteering: A Pilot Study*. CRSP270, Loughborough University.

Gaskin, K. and Fenton, N. (1997) *Blurred Vision: Public Trust in Charities*. Report submitted to the National Council for Voluntary Organisations, London.

Gaskin, K., Vlaeminke, M. and Fenton, N. (1996) *Young People's Attitudes to the Voluntary Sector*. London: National Council for Voluntary Organisations.

Gay, P. (1998) 'Getting into Work: Volunteering for Employability', *Voluntary Action* 1/1: 55–67.

Geertz, C. (1962) 'The Rotating Credit Association: A Middle Rung in Development', *Economic Development and Cultural Change* 10/3: 241–63.

Gellner, E. (1994) *Conditions of Liberty: Civil Society and its Rivals*. London: Hamish Hamilton.

Gellner, E. (1995) 'The Importance of Being Modular', in J. A. Hall (ed.), *Civil Society: Theory, History, Comparison*. Cambridge: Polity.

Gibson, J. (1979) *An Ecological Approach to Visual Perception*. Boston: Houghton Mifflin.

Giddens, A. (1990) *The Consequences of Modernity*. Cambridge: Polity.

Giddens, A. (1991) *Modernity and Self-Identity*. Cambridge: Polity.

Giddens, A. (1992) *The Transformation of Intimacy: Sexuality, Love and Eroticism in Modern Societies*. Cambridge: Polity.

Giddens, A. (1994) 'Risk, Trust and Reflexivity', in U. Beck, S. Lash and A. Giddens (eds), *Reflexive Modernisation*. Cambridge: Polity.

Giddens, A. (1998) *The Third Way: The Renewal of Social Democracy*. Cambridge: Polity.

Gifford, P. (1998) *African Christianity: Its Public Role*. London: Hurst.

Gilarek, K. (1997) 'Coping With the Challenges of Modernity: The Church of England and the Catholic Church in Poland.' Unpublished paper presented to the Fourth International Conference on Religions in CEE, Krakow, 12–14 Dec.

Gilder, G. (1981) *Wealth and Poverty*. London: Bantam Books.

Gill, R. (1992) *Moral Communities*. Exeter: Exeter University Press.

Golding, P. and Middleton, S. (1982) *Images of Welfare*. Oxford: Basil Blackwell.

Granovetter, M. (1973) 'The Strength of Weak Ties', *American Journal of Sociology* 78: 1360–80.

Granovetter, M. (1985) 'Economic Action and Social Structure: The Problem of Embeddedness', *American Journal of Sociology* 19/3: 481–510.

Granovetter, M. and Swedberg, R. (eds) (1992) *The Sociology of Economic Life*. Boulder: Westview Press.

Green, D. and Shapiro, I. (1994) *Pathologies of Rational Choice Theory: A Critique of Applications in Political Science*. New Haven: Yale University Press.

Grice, R. (1999) *Opportunity, Work and Competitiveness: Voluntary Organisations in a Changing Labour Market*. London: NCVO.

Grove-White, R. (1997) 'Brent Spar Rewrote the Rules', *New Statesman*, 20 June.

Grove-White, R., Macnaghten, P., Mayer, S. and Wynne, B. (1997) *Uncertain World: GMOs, Food and Public Attitudes in Britain*. Lancaster: CSEC.

Gutman, A. (ed.) (1998) *Freedom of Association*. Princeton, NJ: Princeton University Press.

Habermas, J. (1987) *Theory of Communicative Action. Vol. 2: Lifeworld and System: A Critique of Functionalist Reason*. Cambridge: Polity.

Habermas, J. (1989) *The Structural Transformation of the Public Sphere*. Cambridge, MA: MIT Press.

Habermas, J. (1990) 'What Does Socialism Mean Today? The Rectifying Revolution and the Need for New Thinking on the Left', *New Left Review* 183: 3–21.

Habermas, J. (1992) *Autonomy and Solidarity: Interviews with Jürgen Habermas*. P. Dews (ed.). London: Verso.

Hall, J. A. (ed.) (1995) *Civil Society: Theory, History, Comparison*. Cambridge: Polity.

Hall, S. (1993) 'Thatcherism Today', *New Statesman and Society* 26, Nov.: 14–16.

Halpern, D. (1998) 'Social Capital, Exclusion and the Quality of Life: Towards a Causal Model and Policy Implications.' Nexus Briefing Document, 31 March.

Hann, C. and Dunne, E. (1996) *Civil Society: Challenging Western Models*. Routledge, London.

Hansmann, H. (1980) 'The Role of Non-profit Enterprise', *Yale Law Journal* 89: 835–901.

Hart, K. (1988) 'Kinship, Contract and Trust: The Economic Organisation of Migrants in an African City Slum', in D. Gambetta (ed.), *Trust: Making and Breaking Cooperative Relations*. Oxford: Basil Blackwell.

Harvey, D. (1989) *The Condition of Postmodernity*. Oxford: Basil Blackwell.

Havel, V. (1993) 'The Post-Communist Nightmare', *New York Review of Books* 27 May.

Havens, J. J., Coutsoukis, P. E. and Schervisch, P. G. (1998) 'Social Participation and Charitable Giving Revisited: Replication of a Multivariate Analysis'. Paper presented to the Annual Conference of the Association for Research on Nonprofit Organizations and Voluntary Action, Seattle, 5–7 Nov.

Hawthorne, G. (1976) *Enlightenment and Despair: A History of Sociology*. Cambridge: Cambridge University Press.

Hayek, F. (1976) *The Mirage of Social Justice*. London: Routledge and Kegan Paul.

Helms, E. (1999) 'Muslim Women's NGOs Between Discourses of Secular Civil Society and Religion-based National Identity in Bošnjak-Majority Areas of Bosnia-Herzegovina.' Unpublished paper presented at *Islam and Human Rights in Post-Communist Europe*, Sofia, 15–16 March.

Hems, L. and Passey, A. (1998) *The UK Voluntary Sector Almanac 1998/99*. London: NCVO.

Henley Centre (1997) *Planning for Social Change 1998*. London: The Henley Centre.

Herbert, D. (1997) *The Common Good in a Plural Society: Muslims, Christians and the Public Arena in Britain*. Unpublished PhD thesis, University of Leeds.

Herbert, D. (2000) 'Virtue Ethics, Justice and Religion in Multicultural Societies', in K. Flanagan and P. Jupp (eds), *Virtue Ethics and Sociology*. London: Macmillan.

Hirst, P. (1994) *Associative Democracy: New Forms of Economic and Social Governance*. Cambridge: Polity Press.

Hirst, P. (1995) 'Can Secondary Associations Enhance Democratic Governance?' in J. Cohen and J. Rogers (eds), *Associations and Democracy*. London: Verso.

HMSO (1998) *Compact Between the Government and the Voluntary Sector*. London: HMSO.

Hodgson, G. (1994) *Economics and Evolution*. Cambridge: Polity.

Hodgkinson, V. A. and Weitzman, M. S. (1996) *Giving and Volunteering in the United States*. Washington, DC: Independent Sector.

Hume, D. (1948) *Treatise on Human Nature*. New York: Macmillan.

Ibrahim, S. (1997) 'From Taliban to Erbakan: The Case of Islam, Civil Society and Democracy', in E. Özdalga and S. Persson (eds), *Civil Society and Democracy in the Muslim World*. Istanbul: Swedish Research Institute.

Izetbegovic, A. (1989) *Islam Between East and West* (2nd edn). Indianapolis: American Trust.

Jackson, F., Bachmeier, M., Wood, J. and Craft, E. (1995) 'Volunteering and Charitable Giving: Do Religious and Associational Ties Promote Helping Behaviour?' *Non-Profit and Voluntary Sector Quarterly* 24/1: 59–78.

Jacobs, J. (1961) *The Death and Life of the Great American Cities*. New York: Random House.

Jacobs, M. (ed.) (1997) *The Greening of the Millennium*. Oxford: Blackwell.

James, E. (1987) 'The Non-profit Sector in Comparative Perspective', in W.W. Powell (ed.) *The Non-profit Sector: A Research Handbook*. New Haven, CT: Yale University Press.

Jamison, A. (1996) 'The Shaping of the Global Environmental Agenda: The Role of Non-governmental Organisations', in S. Lash, B. Szerszynski, and B. Wynne (eds), *Risk, Environment and Modernity*. London: Sage.

Johnson, N., Jenkinson, S., Kendall, I., Bradshaw, Y. and Blackmore, M. (1998) 'Regulating for Quality in the Voluntary Sector', *Journal of Social Policy* 27/3: 307–28.

Johnson, P. (1993) *Frames of Deceit: A Study of the Loss and Recovery of Public and Private Trust.* Cambridge: Cambridge University Press.

Jowell, R., Curtice, J., Park, A., Brook, L., Thomson, K. and Bryson, C. (1997) *British Social Attitudes: The 14th Report.* London: Social and Community Planning Research.

Keane, J. (1988a) *Civil Society and the State.* London: Verso.

Keane, J. (1988b) *Democracy and Civil Society.* London: Verso.

Keane, J. (1998) *Civil Society: Old Images, New Visions.* Cambridge: Polity.

Kee, A. (1990) *Marx and the Failure of Liberation Theology.* London: SCM.

Kendall, J. and Knapp, M. (1996) *The UK Voluntary Sector.* Manchester: Manchester University Press.

Kent, R. A. (1981) *A History of British Empirical Sociology.* Aldershot: Gower.

Knack, S. and Keefer, P. (1995) 'Institutions and Economic Performance: Cross-country Tests Using Alternative Institutional Measures', *Economics and Politics* 7/3: 207–27.

Knight, B. and Stokes, P. (1996) *The Deficit in Civil Society.* The Foundation for Civil Society: Working Paper No. 1.

Kramer, R. (1981) *Voluntary Agencies in the Welfare State.* Berkeley, CA: University of California Press.

Krusche, G. (1994) 'The Church Between Accommodation and Refusal: The Significance of the Lutheran Doctrine of the "Two Kingdoms" for the Churches of the GDR', *Religion, State and Society* 22/3: 324–32.

Kubik, K. (1994) *The Power of Symbols Against the Symbols of Power: The Rise of Solidarity and the Fall of State Socialism in Poland.* University Park, PA: Pennsylvania State University.

Ladd, E. C. (1996) 'The Data Just Don't Show Erosion of America's "Social Capital"', *Public Perspective* 1996: 4–22.

Landry, C. and Mulgan, G. (1995) *The Other Invisible Hand: Remaking Charity for the 21st Century.* London: Demos.

Lane, J., Saxon-Harrold, S. and Weber, N. (1994) *International Giving and Volunteering.* London: Charities Aid Foundation.

Langford, I. H. and McDonald, A-L. (1997) 'Risk Perception, Health and Environmental Change: A Multidimensional Model.' CSERGE Working Paper GEC 97–14, School of Environmental Sciences, University of East Anglia.

Lapidus, I. (1992) 'The Golden Age: The Political Concepts of Islam', *Annals of the American Academy of Religion* 524: 14–15.

Lasch, C. (1995) *The Revolt of the Elites.* New York: Norton.

Lash, S. and Urry, J. (1987) *The End of Organized Capitalism.* Cambridge: Polity Press.

Lash, S. and Urry, J. (1994) *Economies of Signs and Space.* London: Sage.

Lash, S., Szerszynski, B. and Wynne. B. (eds) (1996) *Risk, Environment and Modernity: Towards a New Ecology.* London: Sage.

Leadbeater, C. and Christie, I. (1999) *To Our Mutual Advantage.* London: Demos.

Le Grand, J. (1997) 'Knights, Knaves or Pawns? Human Behaviour and Social Policy', *Journal of Social Policy* 26/2: 149–69.

Lemann, N. (1986) 'The Origins of the Underclass', *The Atlantic Monthly*, June.

Levine, D. (1999) 'Progressive Catholicism, Liberation Theology, and the Challenge of Democracy in Latin America.' Unpublished paper presented to the Politics and Religion Specialist Group of the Political Studies Association, Sheffield, 24 Feb.

Lewis, P. (1993a) 'Beyond Babel: An Anglican Perspective in Bradford', *Islam and Christian-Muslim Relations* 4/1: 118–38.

Lewis, P. (1993b) *Bradford's Muslim Communities and the Reproduction and Representation of Islam.* Unpublished thesis, University of Leeds. Published in modified form as P. Lewis (1994) *Islamic Britain.* London: IB Tauris.

Liebman, C. and Dov-Yehiya, E. (1982) 'Israel's Civil Religion', *Jerusalem Quarterly* 23: 37–69.

Loury, G. (1987) 'Why Should We Care about Group Inequality?' *Social Philosophy and Policy* 5: 249–71.

Luhmann, N. (1979) *Trust and Power.* New York: John Wiley & Sons.

Luhmann, N. (1988) 'Familiarity, Confidence, Trust: Problems and Perspectives', in D. Gambetta (ed.) *Trust: Making and Breaking Co-operative Relations.* Oxford: Basil Blackwell.

Luxmoore, J. and Babiuch, J. (1995a) 'In Search of Faith: The Metaphysical Dialogue Between Poland's Opposition Intellectuals in the 1970s', *Religion, State and Society* 23/1: 75–95.

Luxmoore, J. and Babiuch, J. (1995b) 'In Search of Faith, Part 2: Charter 77 and the Return to Spiritual Values in the Czech Republic', *Religion, State and Society* 23/3: 291–304.

McCormick, J. (1995) *The Global Environmental Movement.* Chichester: Wiley.

MacGill, S. (1987) *The Politics of Anxiety: The Black Inquiry and Childhood Leukemias around Sellafield.* London: Pion.

MacIntyre, A. (1988) *Whose Justice, Which Rationality?* Notre Dame: University of Notre Dame Press.

Macnaghten, P. and Urry, J. (1998) *Contested Natures.* London: Sage.

Macnaghten, P., Grove-White, R., Jacobs, M. and Wynne, B. (1995a) *Public Perceptions and Sustainability: Indicators, Institutions, Participation.* Preston: Lancashire County Council.

Macnaghten, P., Myers, G. and Wynne, B. (1995b) *Public Rhetorics of Environmental Sustainability: Ambivalence and Effects.* Lancaster: CSEC, University of Lancaster.

McSorley, J. (1990) *Living in the Shadow: The People of West Cumbria and the Nuclear Industry.* London: Pluto.

Mandeville, B. (1924) *Fable of the Bees: Or Private Vices, Public Benefits.* Oxford: Clarendon Press.

Marsland, D. (1995) *Self-Reliance.* New Brunswick, NJ: Transaction Books.

Marsland, D. (1996) *Welfare or Welfare State?* London: Macmillan.

Marx, K. (1970) [1843/4] *Critique of Hegel's 'Philosophy of Right'.* J. O'Malley (ed.). Cambridge: Cambridge University Press.

Marx, K. (1977) [1843] 'On the Jewish Question', in *Selected Writings.* D.

McLellan (ed.). Oxford: Oxford University Press.

Melucci, A. (1989) *Nomads of the Present: Social Movements and Individual Needs in Contemporary Society*. J. Keane and P. Mier (eds). London: Hutchinson Radius.

Mestrovic, S. (1993) 'Explaining War in the Land of Medjugorje' in S. Mestrovic, with S. Letica and M. Goreta (eds), *Explaining War in the Land of Medjugorje*. Texas: Texas A&M University Press.

Misztal, B. A. (1996) *Trust in Modern Societies: The Search for the Bases of Social Order*. Cambridge: Polity.

Morrow, V. (1999) 'Conceptualising Social Capital in Relation to the Well-being of Children and Young People: A Critical Review', *The Sociological Review* 47/4: 744–65.

Murray, C. (1984) *Losing Ground: American Social Policy 1950–1980*. New York: Basic Books.

Nagle, R. (1997) *Claiming the Virgin: The Broken Promise of Liberation Theology*. London: Routledge.

Newton, K. (1997) 'Social Capital and Democracy', *American Behavioural Scientist* 40/5: 575–86.

Nino, C. (1989) 'The Communitarian Challenge to Liberal Rights', *Law and Philosophy* 8: 37–52.

Norris, P. (1996) 'Does Television Erode Social Capital? A Reply to Putnam', *PS: Political Science and Politics* 29/3: 474–80.

North, D. (1990) *Institutions, Institutional Change and Economic Performance*. Cambridge: Cambridge University Press.

O'Connell, B. (1999) *Civil Society: The Underpinnings of American Democracy*. New England: Tufts.

Ortmann, A. and Schlesinger, M. (1997) 'Trust, Repute and the Role of Non-profit Enterprises', *Voluntas* 8: 97–199.

Özdalga, E. (1997) 'Civil Society and its Enemies: Reflections on a Debate in the Light of Recent Developments within the Islamic Student Movement in Turkey', in E. Özdalga and S. Persson (eds), *Civil Society and Democracy in the Muslim World*. Istanbul: Swedish Research Institute.

Özdalga, E. and Persson, S. (eds) (1997) *Civil Society and Democracy in the Muslim World*. Istanbul: Swedish Research Institute.

Paine, R. (1970) 'Anthropological Approaches to Friendship', *Humanitas* 6: 139–60.

Passey, A. (1999) *Civil Society in the New Millennium*, Draft report for the Commonwealth Foundation. London: National Council for Voluntary Organisations.

Passey, A. and Hems, L. (1996) *Charity and Lottery: The Competition for Loose Change*. London: National Council for Voluntary Organisations.

Passey, A. and Hems, L. (1997) *Charitable Giving in Great Britain 1996*. London: National Council for Voluntary Organisations.

Passey, A., Hems, L. and Jas, P. (2000) *The UK Voluntary Sector Almanac 2000*. London: National Council for Voluntary Organisations.

Perez-Diaz, R. (1995) 'The Possibility of Civil Society', in J. A. Hall (ed.) *Civil*

*Society: Theory*, History, Comparison. Cambridge: Polity.

Philo, G. And Miller, D. (1997) *Cultural Compliance: Dead Ends of Media/Cultural Studies and Social Science*. Glasgow University: Glasgow Media Group.

Plattner, S. (1989) 'Markets and Marketplaces', in S. Plattner (ed.) *Economic Anthropology*. Stanford, CA: Stanford University Press.

Polanyi, K. (1957) *The Great Transformation*. Boston: Beacon Press.

Polanyi, K. (1992) 'The Economy as an Instituted Process', in M. Granovetter and R. Swedberg (eds), *The Sociology of Economic Life*. Boulder: Westview Press.

Pollack, D. (1995) 'Post Wende Citizens' Movements', in E. Kolinsky, asst. by S. Wilsdorf (eds), *Between Hope and Fear: Everyday Life in Post-Unification East Germany, A Case Study of Leipzig*. Keele: Keele University Press.

Portes, A. and Landolt, P. (1996) 'The Downside of Social Capital', *The American Prospect* 26 (May–June): 18–21.

Potter, D., Goldblatt, D., Kiloh, M. and Lewis, P. (eds) (1997) *Democratization*. Cambridge: Polity.

Powell, F. and Guerin, D. (1997) *Civil Society and Social Policy*. Dublin: A. & A. Farmar.

Przeworski, A. (1991) *Democracy and the Market: Political and Economic Reforms in Eastern Europe and Latin America*. Cambridge: Cambridge University Press.

Putnam, R., with Leonardi, R. and Nanetti, R. (1993a) *Making Democracy Work: Civic Traditions in Modern Italy*. Princeton, NJ: Princeton University Press.

Putnam, R. (1993b) 'What Makes Democracy Work?' *National Civic Review* 82/2: 101–8.

Putnam, R. (1995a) 'Bowling Alone: America's Declining Social Capital', *Journal of Democracy* 6: 65–78.

Putnam, R. (1995b) 'Tuning In, Turning Out: The Strange Disappearance of Social Capital in America', *PS: Political Science and Politics* 28/4: 664–83.

Putnam, R., Pharr, S. and Dalton, R. (2000) *What is Troubling the Trilateral Democracies?* Princeton, NJ: Princeton University Press.

Ratgheb Smith, S. and Lipsky, M. (1993) *Nonprofits for Hire: The Welfare State in an Age of Contracting*. Cambridge, MA: Harvard University Press.

Rhodes, C. and Nabi, N. (1992) 'Brick Lane: A Village Economy in the Shadow of the City?' in L. Budd and S. Whimster (eds), *Global Finance and Urban Living*. London: Routledge.

Roberts, S. (1996) 'Contexts of Charity in the Middle Ages: Religious, Social and Civic', in J. B. Schneewind (ed.), *Giving: Western Ideas of Philanthropy*. Bloomington: Indiana University Press.

Robson, P. (1996) 'Who Owns Voluntary Organisations?' Paper presented to the NCVO Researching the Voluntary Sector Conference, Sept.

Romer, P. (1993) 'Ideas Gaps and Object Gaps in Economic Development', *Journal of Monetary Economics* 32.

Romer, P. (1994) 'The Origins of Endogenous Growth', *Journal of Economic Perspectives* 8/1: 3–22.

Rorty, R. (1996) 'Idealizations, Foundations and Social Practices', in S. Benhabib (ed.), *Democracy and Difference: Contesting the Boundaries of the Political*. Princeton, NJ: Princeton University Press.

Rose, C. (1995) 'Future of Environmental Campaigning', Royal Society of Arts, 6 December.

Rose, N. (1996) 'Governing "Advanced" Liberal Democracies', in A. Barry, T. Osborne and N. Rose (eds), *Foucault and Political Reason: Liberalism, Neo-liberalism and Rationalities of Government*. London: UCL Press.

Ryan, A. (1996) 'The Philanthropic Perspective After a Hundred Years', in J. B. Schneewind (ed.), *Giving: Western Ideas of Philanthropy*. Bloomington: Indiana University Press.

Sacks, J. (1990/1) 'The Persistence of Faith: The 1990 Reith Lectures', *The Listener* 15 Nov. 1990–3 Jan. 1991.

Salamon, L. M. (1994) *The Global Associational Revolution*. London: Demos.

Salamon, L. M. and Anheier, H. K. (1996) *The Emerging Non-Profit Sector*. Manchester: Manchester University Press.

Salamon, L. M. and Anheier, H. K. (1997a) *Defining the Nonprofit Sector: A Cross-national Analysis*. Manchester: Manchester University Press.

Salamon, L. M. and Anheier, H. K. (1997b) 'The Civil Society Sector.' *Society* 34/2.

Salamon, L. M. and Anheier, H. K. (1998) 'Social Origins of Civil Society: Explaining the Non-profit Sector Cross-nationally', *Voluntas* 9/3: 213–49.

Salamon, L. M., Anheier, H. K. and Associates (1998) *The Emerging Sector Revisited: A Summary*. Center for Civil Society Studies, The Johns Hopkins University.

Samuelson, P. A. (1955) *The Foundation of Economics*. Chicago: University of Chicago Press.

Sargeant, A. (1999) 'Charitable Giving: Towards a Model of Donor Behaviour', *Journal of Marketing Management* 15: 215–38.

Schervisch, P. and Havens, J. (1997) 'Social Participation and Charitable Giving: A Multivariate Analysis', *Voluntas* 8: 235–60.

Schneewind, J. B. (ed.) (1996) *Giving: Western Ideas of Philanthropy*. Bloomington: Indiana University Press.

Seligman, A. B. (1992) *The Idea of Civil Society*. Princeton, NJ: Princeton University Press.

Seligman, A. B. (1997) *The Problem of Trust*. Princeton, NJ: Princeton University Press.

Seligman, A. B. (1998a) 'Civil Society: Between Jerusalem and Los Angeles'. Paper presented to the IJPR, London, 7 Sept.

Seligman, A. B. (1998b) 'Theorising Trust and Confidence'. Keynote paper presented to the NCVO Annual Research Conference, Loughborough, 9 Sept.

Sells, M. (1996) 'Religion, History and Genocide in Bosnia-Herzegovina' in G. Davis (ed.), *Religion and Justice in the War Over Bosnia*. London: Routledge.

Shadid, W. and van Koningsveld, S. (eds) (1996) *Muslims in the Margin:*

*Political Response to the Presence of Islam in Western Europe*. Kampen: Kok Pharos.

Shaw, G. K. (1997) 'Policy Implications of Endogenous Growth Theory', in B. Snowdon and H. R. Vane (eds), *A Macroeconomics Reader*. London: Routledge.

Shils, E. (1991) 'The Virtues of Civil Society', *Government and Opposition* 26: 3–20.

Silver, A. (1989) 'Friendship and Trust as Moral Ideas', *European Journal of Sociology* 30: 274–97.

Smart, J. C. C. and Williams, B. (1971) *Utilitarianism For and Against*. Cambridge: Cambridge University Press.

Smelser, N. and Swedberg, R. (eds) (1994) *The Handbook of Economic Sociology*. Princeton, NJ: Princeton University Press.

Squires, P. (1990) *Anti-Social Policy*. Hemel Hempstead: Harvester Wheatsheaf.

Stokes, P. and Knight, B. (1997) 'A Citizens' Charter to Save our Cities', *Independent*, 15 Jan.

Swedberg, R. (1991) 'Major Traditions of Economic Sociology', *Annual Review of Sociology* 17: 251–76.

Szreter, S. (1998) 'A New Political Economy for New Labour: The Importance of Social Capital.' University of Sheffield, Political Economy Research Centre Policy Paper 15.

Sztompka, P. (1998a) 'Trust, Distrust and Two Paradoxes of Democracy', *European Journal of Social Theory* 1/1: 19–32.

Sztompka, P. (1998b) 'Mistrusting Civility: Predicament of a Post-Communist Society', in Alexander, J. C. (ed.) (1998) *Real Civil Societies: Dilemmas of Institutionalization*. London: Sage.

Taylor, C. (1985) 'What is Human Agency?' in *Human Agency and Language*. Cambridge: Cambridge University Press.

Taylor, C. (1989) *Sources of the Self: The Making of Modern Identity*. Cambridge: Cambridge University Press.

Taylor, M. and Lansley, J. (1992) 'Ideology and Welfare in the UK: The Implications for the Voluntary Sector', *Voluntas* 3/2: 153–75.

Taylor-Gooby, P. (1999) 'Markets and Motives: Trust and Egoism in Welfare Markets', *Journal of Social Policy* 28/1: 97–114.

Teeple, G. (1995) *Globalisation and the Decline of Social Reform*. Toronto: Garamond Press.

Tester, K. (1992) *Civil Society*. London: Routledge.

Therborn, G. (1997) 'Beyond Civil Society: Democratic Experiences and their Relevance to the "Middle East"' in E. Özdalga and S. Persson (eds), *Civil Society and Democracy in the Muslim World*. Istanbul: Swedish Research Institute.

Thrift, N. (1993) 'The De-traditionalization of Money and International Financial Centres: The Case of the City of London.' Paper presented to the De-traditionalization Conference, Centre for the Study of Cultural Values, University of Lancaster.

Thrift, N. (1994) 'On the Social and Cultural Determinants of International Finance Centres', in S. Corbridge (ed.), *Money, Space and Power*. Oxford: Blackwell.

Tismaneau, V. (1992) *Reinventing Politics: Eastern Europe After Communism*. New York: Free Press.

Tocqueville, A. de (1969) [1835/40] *Democracy in America*. J. P. Maier (ed.) Garden City: Anchor Books.

Tocqueville, A. de (1988) *The Ancien Regime*, London: Dent & Sons.

Tonkiss, F. (1998) 'Civil/Political', in C. Jenks (ed.), *Core Sociological Dichotomies*. London: Sage.

Tonkiss, F. and Passey, A. (1999) 'Trust, Confidence and Voluntary Organisations: Between Values and Institutions', *Sociology* 33/2: 257–74.

USAID (1999) *Lessons in Implementation: The NGO Story. Building Civil Society in Central and Eastern Europe and the New Independent States*. Washington: USAID.

Uslaner, E. (1996) 'Morality Plays: Social Capital and Moral Behaviour in Anglo-American Democracies'. Paper presented to the Conference on Social Capital in Europe, Milan, Nov.

Uslaner, E. (1997) 'Faith, Hope and Charity: Social Capital, Trust and Collective Action.' University of Maryland, College Park Manuscript.

Walzer, M. (1983) *Spheres of Justice: A Defence of Pluralism*. Oxford: Robertson.

Waters, M. (1995) *Globalization*. London: Routledge.

Wedel, J. (1992) *An Unplanned Society: Poland During and After Communism*. New York: Columbia University Press.

Wedel, J. (1994) 'US Aid to Central and Eastern Europe' in *East-Central Europe Economies in Transition*. Washington: Congress of the United States, US Government Printing Office.

Weisbrod, B.A. (1988) *The Non-profit Economy*. Cambridge, MA: Harvard University Press.

White, G. (1994) 'Civil Society, Democratization and Development (I): Clearing the Analytical Ground', *Democratization* 1/3: 375–90.

Whiteley, P. (1997) 'Economic Growth and Social Capital.' University of Sheffield, Political Economy Research Centre Policy Paper.

Wilkinson, H. and Mulgan, G. (1995) *Freedom's Children: Work, Relationships and Politics for 18–34 Year Olds in Britain Today*. London: Demos.

Williamson, O. E. (1975) *Markets and Hierachies: Analysis and Anti-trust Implications*. New York: Free Press.

Williamson, O. E. (1985) *The Economic Institutions of Capitalism: Firms, Markets, Relational Contracting*. New York: Free Press.

Wilson, W. J. (1996) *When Work Disappears: The World of the New Urban Poor*. New York: Knopf.

Woldring, H. E. S. (1998) 'State and Civil Society in the Political Philosophy of Alexis de Tocqueville', *Voluntas* 9/4: 363–73.

Wolfe, J. (1989) *Whose Keepers? Social Science and Moral Obligation*. Berkeley: University of California Press.

Woolcock, M. (1998) 'Social Capital and Economic Development: Toward a Theoretical Synthesis and Policy Framework', *Theory and Society* 27: 151–208.

Worcester, R. (1994) 'The Sustainable Society: What We Know about What People Think and Do', *Values for a Sustainable Society*, World Environment Day Symposium, June.

Worcester, R. (1995) 'Vital Statistics: Green Gauge of Britain', *BBC Wildlife* 13: 70–3.

Workfare Watch (1996) *Workfare and the Voluntary Sector.* ›http://www.eagle.ca/-nccoa/workfare watch/wrkvol.htm‹

Wuthnow, R. (1998) 'A Reasonable Role for Religion: Moral Practices, Civic Participation and Market Behavior', in R. Hefner (ed.), *Democratic Civility: The Historical and Cross Cultural Possibility of a Modern Political Ideal.* New Brunswick: Transaction Press.

Wynne, B. (1994) 'Scientific Knowledge and the Global Environment', in T. Benton and M. Redclift (eds), *Social Theory and the Global Environment.* London: Routledge.

Wynne, B. (1996) 'May the Sheep Graze Safely', in S. Lash, B. Szerszynski, and B. Wynne (eds), *Risk, Environment and Modernity: Towards a New Ecology.* London: Sage.

Zucker, L. G. (1986) 'Production of Trust: Institutional Sources of Economic Structure, 1840–1920'. *Research in Organizational Behaviour* 8: 53–111.

# Index